URBAN POLICIES IN JAPAN

*A review by the OECD Group on Urban Affairs
undertaken in 1984/5 at the request of the
Government of Japan*

ORGANISATION FOR ECONOMIC CO-OPERATION AND DEVELOPMENT

Pursuant to article 1 of the Convention signed in Paris on 14th December, 1960, and which came into force on 30th September, 1961, the Organisation for Economic Co-operation and Development (OECD) shall promote policies designed:

- to achieve the highest sustainable economic growth and employment and a rising standard of living in Member countries, while maintaining financial stability, and thus to contribute to the development of the world economy;
- to contribute to sound economic expansion in Member as well as non-member countries in the process of economic development; and
- to contribute to the expansion of world trade on a multilateral, non-discriminatory basis in accordance with international obligations.

The Signatories of the Convention on the OECD are Austria, Belgium, Canada, Denmark, France, the Federal Republic of Germany, Greece, Iceland, Ireland, Italy, Luxembourg, the Netherlands, Norway, Portugal, Spain, Sweden, Switzerland, Turkey, the United Kingdom and the United States. The following countries acceded subsequently to this Convention (the dates are those on which the instruments of accession were deposited): Japan (28th April, 1964), Finland (28th January, 1969), Australia (7th June, 1971) and New Zealand (29th May, 1973).

The Socialist Federal Republic of Yugoslavia takes part in certain work of the OECD (agreement of 28th October, 1961).

Publié en français sous le titre:

LES POLITIQUES URBAINES
DU JAPON

Japan is among the most highly urbanised countries in the OECD and the increase in the urban population of Japan in the last 40 years has been larger than the total population of all but two other OECD countries. Following this period of rapid growth, urban Japan is in a transitional phase. In the coming decades it will be confronted not only with the need to cater for continuing urban growth, but with considerable tasks of urban renewal and improving the quality of urban community life. The combination of these linked trends of growth and renewal presents a major challenge to Japanese society.

This Review of Urban Policies in Japan is the first of its kind. In adopting a specifically urban policy perspective, it is recognised that the evolution of urban areas takes place in response to a range of economic and social trends and policies. This is reflected in the wide spectrum of issues covered in the report. The Review was first formally suggested by the Japanese Vice-Minister of Construction at the OECD Group on Urban Affairs meeting at Ministerial Level in 1983. Subsequently, the Review of Urban Policies in Japan was incorporated in the programme of the OECD Group on Urban Affairs.

The policy conclusions, which have been derestricted by the OECD Council, occur at the end of the relevant chapters in the report, but are brought together in the last chapter on urban policy perspectives. The conclusions relate mainly to developing and refining existing urban policies in Japan, rather than making radical departures. The stress is on raising quality and improved targeting. Without an increase of resources it is argued that urban living conditions in Japan by the year 2000 are unlikely to show the degree of improvement necessary to meet the evolving needs of Japanese society.

Also available

MANAGING URBAN CHANGE:

Volume I: Policies and Finance (May 1983)
(97 83 02 1) ISBN 92-64-12442-X   150 pages   £8.50   US$17.00   F85.00   DM38.00

Volume II: The Role of Government (November 1983)
(97 83 04 1) ISBN 92-64-12478-0   114 pages   £5.00   US$10.00   F50.00   DM25.00

To Be Published

REVITALISING URBAN ECONOMIES

MANAGING AND FINANCING URBAN SERVICES

TABLE OF CONTENTS

LIST OF MAPS, DIAGRAMS AND TABLES

LIST OF ABBREVIATIONS

DID	Densely Inhabited District
FILP	Fiscal Investment and Loan Programme
HLC	Housing Loan Corporation
JPIC	Japan Project Industry Council
JHUDC	Japan Housing and Urban Development Corporation
MITI	Ministry of International Trade and Industry
MOC	Ministry of Construction
MREIP	Model Residential Environment Improvement Project
RAIP	Residential Area Improvement Project
UCA	Urbanisation Control Area
UPA	Urbanisation Promotion Area

Note: Superior figures in the text indicate references given at the end of each chapter.

INTRODUCTION

Although country surveys and reviews in various policy areas are a well-established element of the work of the OECD, this Review of Urban Policies in Japan is the first of its kind. Its model is a series of environmental reviews – including one of Japan[1] – carried out by the Organisation, which have recently included chapters on urban policy. However, in adopting a specifically urban policy perspective for this review, it has been recognised that the evolution of urban areas takes place in response to a range of social and economic trends and policies. This is reflected in the wide range of interests, including the urban environment, covered in this report.

The review was first, formally suggested in April 1983 by Mr. Kishiro Nakamura, the Japanese Vice-Minister of Construction, to the OECD Group on Urban Affairs. Meeting at Ministerial level for the first time, the Group agreed that cities are the foundation stones of national economies and the focus of social and economic change, of technical innovation and of large-scale investment and expenditure. Therefore, urban areas have a vital role to play both in the revitalisation of national economies and in the achievement of national, social and environmental objectives. Within this context, Ministers endorsed four priorities for work in the OECD on urban affairs: i) strategies for urban economic development, based on co-operation between different levels of government, public/private sector co-operation and locally-based community initiatives; ii) provision of urban services including improvements in productivity, cost recovery and the introduction of new technology; iii) appropriate objectives for and levels of housing subsidies, taking into account the ability of people to pay for housing and the potential of rehabilitation, to meet housing needs; and iv) operation of land markets, including the re-use of derelict and under-used urban land and the appropriate protection of high quality farm and recreation land.

Following the Ministerial level meeting, further discussions took place at official level within the OECD's Group on Urban Affairs to develop detailed ideas on how the review should be undertaken. In December 1983, on the basis of this further work, the OECD Council decided that the Review of Urban Policies in Japan should be incorporated in the programme of work on urban affairs and set the following four objectives: i) to describe the urban situation, policies and prospects in the reviewed country; ii) to provide an evaluation of the urban policies of the reviewed country; iii) to assist the Government of Japan by making urban policy recommendations; and iv) to assist other OECD countries by identifying comparisons with their own urban trends and policies. These objectives have been used to structure the report, with attention drawn to aspects of Japanese urban policy considered to be of particular interest to other OECD countries.

As well as the importance of this two-way exchange process, the value of Country Reviews is that they allow a comprehensive view to be taken of a specific policy area. The Review of Urban Policies in Japan permits the other projects in OECD's Urban Affairs Programme – on economic development, service provision, housing finance and land markets – to be integrated within the framework of overall national urban policies. As a result

Map 1

JAPAN: REFERENCE MAP

Map 2

THE NATIONAL CAPITAL REGION

*   Tokyo's 23 special wards

the four themes, which reflect the priorities identified by Ministers mentioned in the second paragraph, are strongly represented in the Review. Further, it is hoped that the methodology adopted for the review will be of use to others undertaking similar work.

The first stage of the review process consisted of the preparation by the Japanese Government of a Report[2] which describes and analyses urban trends and policies in Japan. At the same time the OECD Secretariat was assembling a review team of senior policy advisers and consultants with expertise in each of the topics covered by the Government Report (Planning, Finance, Infrastructure, Urban Development, Housing, Land and Urban Economic Development). The Government Report was received in April 1984 and following an analysis of its contents the review team[3] visited Japan in June/July 1984. During the visit the opportunity was taken to see a wide range of urban projects and conditions in Tokaido[4]; and to meet a considerable number of senior politicians and administrators from various Ministries and Local Authorities, as well as academics and representatives of the private sector. The experts also participated in two joint OECD/Japan symposia: one on urban regeneration, in Himeji, the other on public/private co-operation, in Tokyo. Other places visited included Osaka, Kobe, Kyoto, Tsukuba and Tsuchiura.

Following this visit the experts produced a report on their area of expertise, each dealing with a subject identified in the Government Report. These reports were then edited by the OECD Secretariat and formed the basis of the Issues Report[5], the aim of which was to identify the main points on which the OECD and the Japanese Government agreed that the Review should focus. The Report was discussed at the first Review Meeting held in Tokyo in May 1985. At this meeting, opened by the Minister of Construction and chaired by his special adviser, Mr. Moriyuki Sawamoto, a vice chairman of the OECD Group on Urban Affairs, a further opportunity was taken for a discussion between the review team[6] and relevant representatives of Japanese government and society. This meeting agreed upon the key urban policy issues in Japan; the policy areas where changes are required; and the likely direction these changes should follow. The Review Meeting was linked to two symposia – on Urban Management, at Kobe, and on Urban Strategies for the 21st Century, at Tsukuba in Ibaraki Prefecture – and study visits to Yokohama and Kyushu, where the towns visited were Kumamoto, Ohmuta, Yanagawa and Fukuoka.

As a result of the Review Meeting the policy recommendations which form the basis of this Report were formulated. The Report's conclusions were approved by the OECD Group on Urban Affairs at its sixth session in January 1986, when a final exchange of views took place between the experts and Japanese Government officials. Subsequently the OECD Council agreed to derestrict the conclusions and the Secretary General agreed to the publication of the full report.

The Government of Japan gave considerable and thorough support to the Review throughout its course. The OECD is deeply appreciative of the resources devoted to the Review both by the Government of Japan and the other Member governments which contributed to the review process, as well as the Committee, presided over initially by Mr. Mitsuyoshi Maeda and later by Mr. Ryouichiro Tsurumi, set up by private sector firms in Japan for the promotion of the country review.

NOTES AND REFERENCES

1. *Environmental Policies in Japan*, OECD, Paris, 1977.

2. *Government Report on Urban Problems and Policies in Japan*, Ministry of Construction, Tokyo, 1984.

3. T. Britton (United States), Chairman of the OECD Group on Urban Affairs, S. Jussil (Sweden), M. Logan (Australia), R. Mabey (United Kingdom), J-E. Roullier (France), G. Town (New Zealand), S. Trollegaard (Denmark), H. Wollmann (Germany), H. Yap (Netherlands), J. Alden, N. Glickman, R. Kirwan (Consultants) and J. Zetter (Secretariat).

4. Tokaido is the urbanised south coast of central Honshu, including a range of towns and cities but also the three largest metropolitan areas: the National Capital Region (based on Tokyo) to the east, Kinki (based on Osaka) to the west, with Chubu (based on Nagoya) between them (Map 1). The Tokyo region is variously defined in the literature (e.g. Keihin, Kanto). In the Report references to the Tokyo metropolitan area imply the National Capital region (Map 2). Similarly, references to the Osaka and Nagoya metropolitan areas refer to Kinki and Chubu respectively. When the city of Tokyo is mentioned this refers to the area covered by the 23 special wards which comprise the city centre and inner suburbs. References to Osaka and Nagoya, and other cities, refer to the municipal government units concerned.

5. *Review of Urban Policies in Japan: Issues Report*, Urban Affairs Division, Environment Directorate, OECD, Paris, 1984.

6. Some changes took place in the team compared with the first visit. In particular B. Birgersson (Sweden) and D. Stroud (United Kingdom), Vice Chairmen of the OECD Group on Urban Affairs, C. Hemmer (Luxembourg), Chairman of the OECD Project Group on Housing Finance and E. Lykke, Director of the Environment Directorate, OECD, joined the review team. E. Crotto acted as Secretary to the team.

Chapter 1

URBAN JAPAN IN TRANSITION

A. Defining Urban Policies

All levels of government and many governmental and non-governmental agencies are involved in formulating and implementing urban policies. This review concentrates on the role of national government, although attention is also drawn to the influence it can exert, often through other agencies and the private sector, on policy implementation. National urban policies are framed in terms of two distinct but related aspects of the development process. First, they pursue the objective of guiding the location of urban develoment. Secondly, urban policies seek to influence the character of urban development and redevelopment. Hence, the essence of urban policies is that they are targetted and spatial.

These characteristics make urban policies valuable weapons in the policy armoury at a time when some of the major social and economic challenges facing OECD societies are highly concentrated, often in combination, in cities. An urban perspective can take into account the individual characteristics of specific population groups, for example the unemployed, located in particular parts of cities, and the needs of specific cities, for example for improved services. Urban policies can coordinate resources and direct programmes to where they are most needed and can have the most significant effect.

Because the built environment tends to change more slowly than economic and social behaviour, cities can be a barrier to change unless emerging needs are taken into account when development and redevelopment takes place. Urban policies can, therefore, play a crucial role in the restructuring of the productive capacity of OECD Member countries. As seed beds of interchange, creation and innovation, cities both influence and are influenced by the processes of change. For example, macro-economic policies to maintain employment, to be successful nationally, often need to be supported at the labour market scale, which usually coincides with a metropolitan area. The targetted and spatial nature of urban policies is also a vital ingredient and complement of other national policies for realising the opportunities and confronting the challenges presented by social and economic change.

Cities embody the cultural values of a society and have been built in all time periods and in all parts of the globe. This universality of the urban phenomenon gives the topic of urban policies a particular aptness for comparative, international study. However, despite their generic qualities, national patterns of urbanisation and individual cities are in their particular characteristics, a reflection of the social values and economic life of the country concerned. In any international discussion of urban policies a note of warning, therefore, needs to be sounded: care has to be taken in transferring policy prescriptions for cities from one country to another.

14

Diagram 1

URBANISATION IN OECD COUNTRIES, 1950-1980

Population in urban areas as a percentage of total population[1]

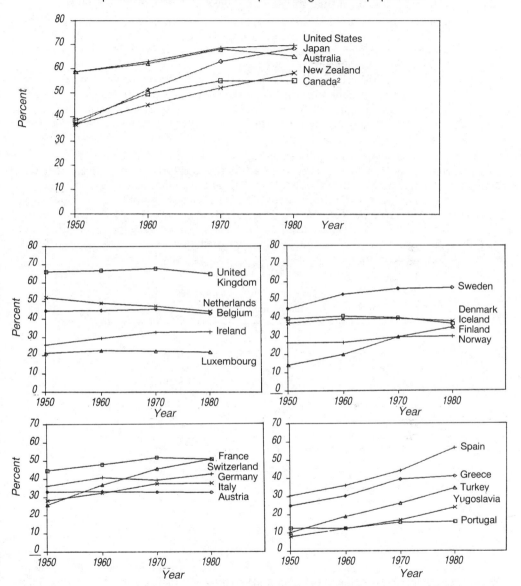

Notes : 1. *Urban population is defined as the population in urban areas of 50 000 or more inhabitants. International comparisons should be treated with caution due to a number of differences in definitions of urban area and urban population between countries and over time.*

2. *The trend line for Canada has been calculated by the Secretariat on the basis of partial data.*

Source : *OECD.*

15

B. Urban Japan

There is a developing interest in the economic performance of Japan, particularly as it has managed to avoid high unemployment, inflation and interest rates[1]. However, three specific reasons contribute to the opportune timing of a review of Japanese urban policies:

i) The high level of urbanisation in Japan indicates that urban policies have recently become more influential for the future economic and social wellbeing of the Japanese people and, therefore, the choice made between alternative policy options becomes more significant;

ii) The nature of the urban policy challenges in Japan is changing as the need for urban redevelopment is added to continuing concerns to deal with urban growth; and

iii) The nature of urban development policy is changing from catering for rural to urban migration to dealing with migration from densely populated urban centres to suburban areas.

Japan is among the most highly urbanised countries in the OECD (Diagram 1). This level of urbanisation has mostly been reached in the last forty years and is expected to continue, although at a reduced rate (Table 1). This combination of recent and rapid urbanisation has brought with it two related policy challenges. First, the need to incorporate an urban perspective in the formulation of government policy and, secondly, to begin to reorientate urban policies away from an exclusive concern with regulating urban growth, towards policies concerned with managing the urban areas that have been so quickly developed in the recent past.

Table 1.   **Urban population in Japan 1920-2000**
Millions and Percentage

Year	National population	Urban population
1920	55.4	10.1 (18)
1930	64.4	15.4 (24)
1940	73.1	27.6 (38)
1950	84.1	31.4 (37)
1960[1]	93.4	40.8 (44)
1970	103.7	55.5 (54)
1980	117.1	69.9 (60)
1990	127.2	85.6 (67)
2000	135.0	96.6 (72)

1. Definition of urban changed from those living in cities to those living in the Densely Inhabited Districts (DIDs)[2].
Source: Government Report.

This is not to say that the running of large urban areas is something new for the Japanese people: there is a long tradition to build on. In the 16th century Tokyo, with an estimated one million inhabitants, was the largest city in the world and in 1700 Osaka was probably third in the world urban hierarchy after London. Again today, with approximately 30 million people, the Tokyo Metropolitan Area, as opposed to the city of Tokyo, is the largest in the world. Nor does the need for a change of emphasis in its urban policies imply that Japan has handled this

16

rapid process of urbanisation, associated with industrialisation, less well than other countries. Considering the scale and rate of urban development in Japan in the last 40 years, considerable resourcefulness has characterised the approach taken to formulating and implementing urban policy.

The increase in the urban population of Japan in the last 40 years has been larger than the total population of all but two other OECD countries. In the 1950-1980 period this increase occurred at the third fastest rate (Table 2). In the light of the urban challenges implied in these figures, Japan has achieved a high level of urbanisation through government policies mostly taking the form of supporting framework legislation and direct intervention in the development process. However, the very rapidity of development, combined with changing needs and demands, inevitably means that Japanese cities and towns display features which are capable of improvement. Further, with another 18 million urban residents to be housed by the year 2000 – nearly two more cities the size of Tokyo – the urban policy challenges in Japan will not diminish. By 1990 the area of DIDs is expected to increase to 12 900 km^2 as compared to 11 810 km^2 in 1985.

Table 2. **Urban population in OECD countries[1] 1950-1980[2]**

Thousands and Percentage

Countries[3]	1950	1960	1970	1980	Average annual rate of change 1950-1980 (%)
Turkey	2 119	4 655	8 307	15 251	6.80
Yugoslavia	1 258	2 284	3 450	5 332	4.47
Japan	27 347	48 291	65 480	80 175	3.65
Finland	572	883	1 335	1 657	3.61
New Zealand	716	1 088	1 494	1 852	3.22
Canada[4]	5 380	9 060	11 880	13 420	3.09
Spain	8 625	10 925	14 959	19 385	2.65
Greece	1 908	2 539	3 444	3 997	2.50
Australia	5 271	6 542	8 689	9 508	2.21
Switzerland	1 740	2 005	2 854	3 243	2.10
United States	89 317	112 885	139 419	158 000	1.92
Italy	13 377	16 415	20 237	21 322	1.57
France	18 353	20 757	24 935	27 647	1.37
Ireland	763	831	976	1 140	1.35
Iceland	57	72	82	84	1.30
Sweden	3 185	3 974	4 519	4 690	1.30
Portugal	1 065	1 106	1 352	1 559	1.28
Germany	18 340	23 001	23 881	26 338	1.21
Norway	867	949	1 133	1 210	1.12
Luxembourg	62	72	76	80	0.83
Denmark	1 571	1 801	1 944	1 942	0.71
Netherlands	5 200	5 558	6 127	6 246	0.61
United Kingdom	32 224	35 098	36 311	36 186	0.39
Belgium	3 894	4 104	4 395	4 245	0.03
Austria	2 288	2 480	2 546	2 473	0.26
Total OECD	245 499	317 375	389 825	446 982	2.03

1. Population in urban areas or municipalities of 50 000 or more inhabitants.
2. Or nearest available years.
3. Ranked by average annual rate of change.
4. Secretariat estimates based on partial data.
Source: OECD, National Yearbooks and Statistical Yearbooks.

Urbanisation is a process through which societies are transformed and urban areas are, therefore, in a continuous state of flux. Further, the existing national system of cities and towns itself influences the direction and pace of change in society. Following a 40 year period of rapid growth, urban Japan is in a transitional phase. In the coming decades it will be confronted not only with the need to cater for continuing urban growth but with considerable challenges of urban renewal and improving the quality of urban community life. The combination of these linked challenges of growth and renewal will involve a major task for Japanese society.

This introduces the second and third factors that make a review of urban policies in Japan particularly opportune. Besides the opportunity to begin to switch policy priorities from the quantity of urban growth that is required to the quality of the urban environment, there is an additional need to realise that the major part of the urban development in Japan in the year 2000 and beyond is already built. An ageing physical stock is as important a consideration for the future of Japan as its ageing population structure.

Thus in the past forty years a certain degree of flexibility existed about where urban development could take place. This adaptability is part of the explanation for the dynamic performance of the Japanese economy, as younger people moved from low productivity employment in agriculture to manufacturing establishments in urban areas. The new migration pattern in Japan is likely to be of existing urban residents to suburban areas and smaller towns in the major metropolitan areas, in search of a higher standard of accommodation and amenity. Since 1970 the cities of Tokyo and Osaka have lost population while their metropolitan areas have continued to grow. In the period 1975-80 the largest cities in Japan grew by only 0.3 per cent compared to a national population growth rate of 4.6 per cent (Table 3).

Table 3. **Population growth in Tokyo and designated cities[1]**

Thousands and Percentage

Towns	1975	1980	1983	1970-75	1975-80
Tokyo (23 Wards)	8 647	8 349	8 170	−2.2	−3.4
Yokohama	2 622	2 774	2 915	17.1	5.8
Osaka	2 779	2 648	2 534	−6.8	−4.7
Nagoya	2 080	2 083	2 066	2.1	0.4
Kyoto	1 461	1 473	1 479	3.0	0.8
Sapporo	1 241	1 402	1 464	22.8	13.0
Kobe	1 361	1 367	1 381	5.6	0.5
Fukuoka	1 002	1 089	1 098	15.0	8.6
Kitakyushu	1 058	1 065	1 052	1.5	0.6
Kawasaki	1 015	1 041	1 049	4.3	2.5
Hiroshima	853	899	907	14.2	5.5
Total	24 119	24 190	24 115	2.8	0.3

1. Rank order by 1983 population.
Source: Ministry of Construction.

Now that the period of rural to urban migration is drawing to its close, the other dimension of the changing perspective is the increasing competition between cities in a "zero sum" game. The population of Japan is due to stabilise in 20 years time. Osaka and, to a lesser extent, Nagoya are losing functions to Tokyo and smaller cities are tending to gain at the expense of larger ones. With a centralised system, this will increase pressure on the national government to intervene as an arbitrator when particular cities are adversely affected by changes in the distribution of urban functions.

Six types of urban area in Japan have been experiencing population decline:

  i) Where business development is displacing residential use (e.g. Tokyo);
  ii) Where industry is decentralising (Amagasaki);
  iii) Dormitory towns with sub-standard housing (Tanashi);
  iv) Cities relying on heavy industry (Nemuro);
  v) Cities based on primary industry in remote locations (Kumano); and
  vi) Traditional holiday resorts (Nikko).

The combination of the falling numbers of new migrants and the process of urban deconcentration could lead to more widespread inner city decline, as experienced in some European and North American cities. This is not an imminent possibility but does emphasise the importance of urban revitalisation policies in the larger Japanese cities.

The degree of potential flexibility over the location and rate of new urban development is being reduced. For this reason, particularly because the land area is so constrained in relation to Japan's population (Chapter 4), the urban policy options are becoming considerably more confined than hitherto. Therefore, it becomes of higher priority to ensure that future urban policies make the maximum use of the limited space – metaphorically and physically speaking – available for policy manoeuvre. Future adaptations of Japanese society to new social and economic circumstances will, to a large extent, have to be accommodated either within or at the margin of the existing system of urban settlements.

C. Urban Policy Objectives

In reviewing policies it is a useful exercise to consider their stated objectives. This process helps both in evaluating the success of current policies and suggesting alternatives for the future. The most comprehensive set of Japanese urban policy objectives is to be found in the first chapter of the City Planning Act, 1968. The key phrases in the official English translation of Articles 1 and 2, within the general and unquantifiable aim of achieving "sound development and systematic improvement of cities", are:

  i) "Balanced development of the country";
  ii) "Rational utilisation of land";
  iii) "Healthy and cultured urban life"; and
  iv) "Promotion of public welfare".

In commenting more generally on urban policy objectives in Japan the switch from quantity and growth to quality and stability has been noted by other commentators[3]. Also, in examining a wide range of current plans for Japanese urban areas the objectives mentioned above are fully echoed.

These four interlinked and quantifiable objectives have been used to structure the report. Following this introductory chapter, because urban policies interact strongly with other government policies the general context for urban policies in Japan is reviewed (Chapter 2). Attention is then turned to the question of balanced development in Japan (Chapter 3), because urban concentration is the key to understanding the nature of the urban policy challenges facing the government.

Next, attention is turned to policies for the rational use of land (Chapter 4). Japan is not a natural resource rich country and the scale and nature of its land surface is the major influence on urban policies. The next of the four objectives mentioned above relates generally to healthy and cultured urban life. Policies for the improvement of housing are, therefore, the next subject for analysis (Chapter 5) linked to the public welfare objective. As a highly urbanised nation the quality of urban facilities plays a larger than average part in the welfare of the Japanese people. The government is concerned to turn the benefits of economic growth into an improved standard of urban public stock in Japan and these policy topics are then considered (Chapter 6) together with related financial questions (Chapter 7). Finally, linked to the provision of infrastructure and the promotion of public welfare as well as a "healthy" urban life, the question of urban amenities is discussed (Chapter 8).

The policy conclusions occur in the relevant chapters but they are brought together in a chapter on urban policy perspectives (Chapter 9). The conclusions relate mainly to developing and refining existing urban policies in Japan, rather than making radical departures. The stress is on raising quality, improved targetting and finding more resources from within the urban sector. The changing urban context is also reflected as the needs switch to regulating urban sprawl in Metropolitan Japan and managing the existing urban environment. The question of devoting more national resources to urban improvement implies less resources for other sectors of the economy. This is a matter which is for the Japanese Government to consider and goes beyond the scope of an urban policy review. However, without an increase of resources it can be said that urban living conditions in Japan by the year 2000 are unlikely to show the degree of improvement necessary to meet the evolving needs of Japanese society.

In this connection, the Review of Urban Policies was given an added dimension in its concluding stages by the publication of the 1984/5 OECD survey of the Japanese economy. This concluded that encouraging residential construction would help achieve a better balance between domestic savings and investment, a more sustainable growth pattern in the Japanese economy and more equilibrium in international current account balances. "Consideration might also be given to encouraging residential construction through greater availability of mortgage funds and easier terms of access to financing. Reforms of the extensive regulations that govern construction would be a key adjunct to such policies. Also necessary would be increases in land use taxation to eliminate the preferential treatment given to lightly-used agricultural land in suburban areas; this change of taxation would promote a more efficient use of scarce land resources"[4]. Thus the conclusions of this urban policy review report can be seen very much as a way of refining this general economic advice, relating the development of urban policy directly to major questions of encouraging the stable development of the world economy.

In October 1985, an action programme of economic measures to expand domestic demand was announced by the Japanese Government which emphasised the improvement of social capital and the expansion of opportunities for private investment. Specific measures in the urban development field included:

i) Raising by 4 per cent the loan ceiling of the Housing Loan Corporation (HLC) from 490 000 to 510 000 units per annum;
ii) Increasing the amount of HLC loan per housing unit;
iii) The release of public sector land for development;
iv) The removal of certain regulations in the planning and building fields; and
v) Additional financial allocations for infrastructure expenditure.

The Review of Urban Policies in Japan provides the wider context for the general policy of the Government to expand domestic demand.

D.   Policy Conclusions

National urban policy aims to influence the location and quality of urban development and redevelopment. An urban perspective is particularly useful for integrating and targetting policies, particularly as cities are at the forefront of meeting the challenges and realising the opportunities arising from social and economic changes. This approach is recognised in Japan and the objectives of the City Planning Act, 1968 – to secure balanced development, the rational use of land, the promotion of public welfare and a healthy and cultured urban life – are a useful yardstick both to evaluate past performance and set priorities for future urban policies.

Japan is now a highly urbanised country and is destined to become more so, but this is not firmly established in the national consciousness. Because this high level of urbanisation has been achieved in a comparatively short period, it is not fully recognised in all spheres of government policy making. At the same time, two changes in the nature of the challenges facing urban policy makers are yet to be adequately recognised. First, a continuing need to cater for urban growth has to be balanced against the need for revitalisation in the urban areas so rapidly expanded in the past 40 years. Secondly, while the agricultural sector in Japan is still comparatively large, future urban development demands will come more from the natural increase of the existing urban population linked to the process of urban deconcentration than from rural to urban migration, as in the past.

An additional contextual point of significance is the increasing difficulty and importance of making the right choice from amongst the urban policy options that are available. Most of urban Japan in the year 2000 is already built. At the same time, with falling rates both of national population growth and rural to urban migration, the development and redevelopment of one urban area will increasingly be at the expense of another. Although the overall shortage of good development land in Japan may prevent it occurring, the situation raises the risk of population and employment decline in those cities which are less well placed to compete.

Not only may increased inter-city competition lead to more central government involvement in urban policy, but the new link being made between urban development and stimulating domestic demand will make this involvement more likely. The Japanese government has now recognised the close link between domestic demand and the development and improvement of urban areas. To be effective, this will need to be reinforced by giving higher priority to urban policy and increasing the resources available to upgrade housing and overhead social capital in Japanese cities.

NOTES AND REFERENCES

1. *Japanese Urban Planning: Some British Perspectives* (Introduction I. Masser), Department of Town and Regional Planning, University of Sheffield, 1985.

2. DID is the most commonly used index of urbanisation in Japan. It was first used in the 1960 census and is defined as a district which has a population of more than 5 000 and a density of 4 000 or more people per Km^2.

3. *Economic and Regional Policy in Post War Japan*, N. Glickman and A. Tani, Lyndon B. Johnson School of Public Affairs, University of Texas, 1984.

4. *Economic Surveys 1984/1985: Japan*, OECD, Paris, 1985.

Chapter 2

THE CONTEXT FOR URBAN POLICY

A. Economic Performance

Before moving on to an analysis of specific urban policies in Japan, in the light of the objectives taken from the City Planning Act 1968, set out in the previous chapter, the wider policy context needs to be considered. This covers related areas of policy which, while not specifically urban in their intentions, express other aims of government which directly affect urbanisation trends. This is particularly important in the case of urban policy which, because it has a spatial rather than a sectoral outlook, seeks to integrate other policies in a targetted way.

As has been mentioned, the OECD publishes annual economic surveys and outlooks for Member countries[1] and it is not within the scope of a review of urban policies to cover much of the same ground in respect of Japan. However, there are certain, interlinked features of the Japanese economy that have a particular influence on the form and location of urban development and redevelopment. Economic policies, therefore, interact closely with urban policies. In order to understand the reasons for the more detailed policy conclusions set out later in this Report these contextual features need to be highlighted.

The overall performance of the Japanese economy is widely known. The "virtuous circle"[2] of a sustainable growth rate combined with, by international standards, low inflation, relatively low interest rates and low unemployment has been maintained in recent years. In comparison with the late 1950s and 1960s, the 1970s and 1980s have seen annual growth rates of GDP in Japan cut by half – from 10 per cent to 5 per cent. However this is still a high rate compared to other OECD countries and, even in the light of the reduction, it cannot be effectively argued that the overall financial resources are not available, in both the public and private sector, to improve considerably the urban service, environmental and infrastructure standards in Japanese cities.

It will be a matter of political priority whether the Japanese Government chooses to secure the allocation of resources to urban improvement objectives. The link to domestic demand has been referred to and it is argued, later in the Report, that there would be good economic as well as social and environmental reasons for doing so. But there are political constraints which need to be recognised. Electoral boundaries have not been redrawn to reflect the rapid rate of rural to urban migration in recent decades. However, the declaration by the Supreme Court that the 1983 election was unconstitutional[3] may speed the process of boundary reform, in which a maximum disparity of 5:1 occurs between certain urban and rural constituencies in the number of votes needed to elect a Diet member.

Within the overall perspective of a growing economy, able if it were so decided to devote increasing resources to improving the quality of urban services and facilities, the public sector indebtedness in Japan is comparatively high. The value of government bonds issued rose considerably, from Y 15 trillion to Y 122 trillion between 1975 and 1984. This results partially from the high expenditure in the 1970s when public spending, much of it on urban infrastructure and services, was used to maintain economic growth in the wake of the oil shocks. It was in 1975 that deficit financing bonds were first issued and, by 1979, 40 per cent of the general account budget was financed by bond issues. However, this situation is being brought under control, with annual budget deficits in the order of 5 per cent of GNP.

While the size of the public sector debt in Japan, 69 per cent of GNP, is important because it is from the public sector that most expenditure on overhead social capital comes, the size of the public sector itself is an important economic consideration for urban improvement programmes. Considering its stage of development and the generally low level of infrastructure provision, in 1983 Japan had the lowest ratio among OECD countries of public expenditure to GDP (Table 4)[4]. However, within the public expenditure total the proportion allocated to capital investment is the highest among OECD countries.

Table 4. **Government final consumption expenditure as a percentage of GDP, OECD countries, 1960-1983**

Percentage

Countries[1]	1960	1970	1980	1983
Sweden	15.8	21.4	28.8	28.5
Denmark	13.3	20.0	26.7	27.2
United Kingdom	16.4	17.6	21.3	22.0
Canada	13.6	19.2	19.5	21.0
Ireland	12.5	14.6	20.3	20.2
Germany	13.4	15.8	20.1	20.0
Italy	12.8	13.8	16.4	19.5
Norway	12.9	16.9	18.8	19.5
Finland	11.9	14.7	18.1	19.4
United States	16.9	19.2	18.3	19.3
Greece	11.7	12.6	16.4	18.8
Austria	13.0	14.7	18.0	18.7
Belgium	12.4	13.4	18.0	17.7
Netherlands	12.8	15.6	17.9	17.7
Australia	9.4	12.2	16.5	17.6
Luxembourg	9.8	10.7	16.7	17.3
New Zealand	10.7	13.2	17.0	17.0
France	13.0	13.4	15.2	16.3
Portugal	10.5	13.8	14.4	14.6
Switzerland	8.8	10.5	12.7	13.5
Iceland	8.5	9.7	11.7	12.3
Spain	7.4	8.5	11.5	12.3
Turkey	10.5	12.9	12.6	10.8
Japan	8.0	7.4	10.0	10.2
Total OECD	15.0	16.4	17.7	17.8

1. Ranked by percentage share in 1983.
Source: OECD.

The Japanese Government's fiscal policy to reduce the public deficit is by holding public expenditure level, while at the same time tax revenues increase from the overall growth in the economy. The national public works budget was cut by 2.3 per cent in 1985, following on from

23

a 2.0 per cent reduction in 1984. The Fiscal Investment and Loan Programme (FILP) was cut in 1985, for the first time since 1954, but the FILP funds for public works institutions were increased by 7.1 per cent from the previous year. In contrast the Local Finance Plan envisages a 5 per cent growth in local authority spending. Thus the total amount of resources for public works projects is higher than in 1984. This approach has already allowed the level of local government debt to be brought within reasonable limits, following the high levels of the 1970s and early 1980s.

Mention was made earlier, in relation to the level of the public sector debt, of the high savings ratio which is a particular feature of the Japanese economy. The reasons for this lie in the high level of personal savings based on a tradition of individual provision for retirement and ill health; the recent reductions in public sector expenditure; and the maturing of the Japanese economy and the consequent reduced demand for large scale industrial investment. Nevertheless, changes are taking place from a situation in which private household savings flowed through intermediaries to the corporate sector to finance industrial reinvestment, to one where private sector surpluses are absorbed by bonds to finance the public sector deficit[5]. In 1970 18.2 per cent of GDP was saved and although this has stabilised in recent years, by international standards the levels are comparatively high (Table 5). Private consumption in Japan, which is the other side of the coin, remains low, 15th in OECD (Table 6).

Table 5.   **Net household saving as a percentage of disposable household income, OECD countries, 1960-1983**

Percentage

Countries[1]	1960	1970	1980	1983	
Portugal	..	14.0	30.2	28.5	(1981)
Italy	16.5	18.9	20.5	20.4	(1982)
Japan	17.4	18.2	19.2	17.3	
Belgium	10.6	17.1	15.3	16.5	
Greece	7.3	16.0	24.2	16.5	(1982)
Canada	3.9	6.1	12.9	13.5	
Netherlands	14.4	14.0	10.9	13.0	
Switzerland	8.6	13.6	9.9	12.5	
Australia	9.3	11.1	12.8	12.1	(1982)
France	11.5	12.9	11.4	11.5	
Germany	8.6	13.8	12.8	11.4	
Finland	3.9	4.9	7.2	8.1	
Spain	8.0	10.6	7.4	7.8	(1981)
United States	7.0	9.8	8.0	7.0	
Austria	10.5	11.9	9.9	7.0	
United Kingdom	4.5	5.9	11.3	6.7	
Sweden	7.7	4.2	5.2	5.0	(1981)
Luxembourg	..	..	12.4	..	
Denmark	..	..	..	..	
Iceland	..	..	..	..	
Ireland	..	..	..	..	
New Zealand	..	..	..	..	
Norway	..	..	..	..	
Turkey	..	..	..	..	
Total OECD[2]	8.2	11.5	12.0	10.1	

1. Ranked by percentage share in 1983.
2. Partial totals.
Source: OECD.

Table 6. **Private final consumption expenditure as a percentage of GDP, OECD countries, 1960-1983**

Percentage

Countries[1]	1960	1970	1980	1983
Turkey	75.8	70.0	73.6	73.8
Spain	71.6	68.0	69.8	69.3
Portugal	73.1	65.9	66.6	69.2
Greece	80.3	69.2	64.0	66.6
United States	63.8	62.8	64.3	66.2
Belgium	69.2	59.8	63.5	65.2
France	61.9	60.0	63.0	64.2
Iceland	66.6	64.5	60.5	63.3
Switzerland	62.4	59.0	63.6	62.7
Italy	62.7	62.6	61.5	62.5
Australia	65.7	60.7	60.2	62.1
Luxembourg	55.2	51.3	58.5	61.4
Netherlands	58.2	58.1	61.1	60.5
United Kingdom	66.3	62.0	59.2	60.3
Japan	58.9	52.2	58.3	59.4
New Zealand	68.6	63.3	59.5	59.3
Ireland	76.6	68.9	65.2	59.0
Austria	59.6	54.6	55.5	57.8
Germany	56.8	54.6	56.3	56.8
Denmark	62.0	57.4	55.9	54.5
Finland	60.8	57.6	54.0	54.2
Canada	65.2	57.5	55.4	53.6
Sweden	60.0	53.6	51.8	51.9
Norway	59.2	53.9	47.4	47.9
Total OECD	63.4	60.3	61.2	62.7

1. Ranked by percentage share in 1983.
Source: OECD.

There is a close relationship between housing and the level of personal savings, because the affordability of housing is related to the amount of personal savings that can be accumulated. One of the reasons behind the predicted fall in the savings ratio is that higher home ownership figures will reduce the number of households needing to save for house purchase. Another link between finance policy and the urban development situation is also important. The capital market investment opportunities in Japan have in the past made an equity stake in land of considerable value, because of its superiority in capital gains terms to postal and other savings. However, this situation is changing as land prices stabilize and the other opportunities for investment both inside and outside Japan are increasing.

Besides house purchase there are a number of other factors which influence the high savings propensity in Japan. Saving for retirement and higher education are important, as are the bonus payment system and the exemption from tax of most household interest income on savings. These savings, together with the cash flow into national pension fund schemes, are channelled into low interest loans to finance development by public corporations, including the Housing Loan Corporation (Chapter 5), local government and public development banks. Thus a source of funds for urban investment exists, which could be readily expanded.

The key will be to find policies which promote domestic demand, while assisting the maintenance of current levels of economic performance by substituting for export based growth. An increase in the short term in capital investment by the public sector would be a practical way of improving the quality of urban areas. There are no severe constraints to urban investment, in terms of the performance of the economy. Further, the mechanisms exist for channelling low interest investment into the upgrading of urban infrastructure, housing and services. These points are returned to later when the general question of financing urban infrastructure is considered (Chapter 7).

B. Changing Industrial Structure

One issue, where a close relationship can be deduced between economic and urban trends, concerns changes between different sectors of the economy. Japan has been experiencing the same development of the tertiary sector of its economy as other comparable countries (Table 7). This sector has grown from 41 per cent to 54 per cent between 1960 and

Table 7.   **Civilian employment by sector, OECD countries, 1970-1980**

Percentage

Countries[1]	Agriculture[2]			Industry[3]			Services[4]		
	1970	1980	% Change 1970-80	1970	1980	% Change 1970-80	1970	1980	% Change 1970-1980
United States	3 567	3 529	−1.1	27 029	30 313	12.1	48 083	65 461	36.1
Japan	8 860	5 770	−34.9	18 190	19 560	7.5	23 890	30 030	25.7
United States	787	647	−17.8	10 908	9 424	−13.6	12 686	14 912	17.5
Germany	2 262	1 436	−36.5	12 679	11 383	−10.2	11 228	12 952	15.4
France	2 753	1 854	−32.7	7 973	7 656	−4.0	9 602	11 837	23.3
Italy	3 878	2 899	−25.2	7 591	7 699	1.4	7 749	9 715	25.4
Canada	604	583	−3.5	2 449	3 055	24.7	4 866	7 070	45.3
Spain	3 310	2 122	−35.9	4 335	4 058	−6.4	4 575	5 074	10.9
Australia	432	408	−5.6	1 992	1 937	−2.8	2 964	3 897	31.5
Turkey	8 506	8 820	3.7	1 826	2 352	28.8	2 251	3 359	49.2
Netherlands	289	246	−14.9	1 821	1 562	−14.2	2 569	3 165	23.2
Sweden	314	237	−24.5	1 480	1 363	−7.9	2 060	2 631	27.7
Belgium	174	112	−35.6	1 537	1 277	−16.9	1 947	2 354	20.9
Austria	445	295	−33.7	1 301	1 315	1.1	1 329	1 664	25.2
Switzerland	269	218	−19.0	1 433	1 191	−16.9	1 422	1 607	13.0
Denmark	266	175	−34.2	876	749	−14.5	1 173	1 536	30.9
Portugal	1 004	1 120	11.6	1 101	1 412	28.2	1 240	1 393	12.3
New Zealand	130	138	6.2	424	426	0.5	1 240	1 393	12.3
Greece	1 279	1 016	−20.6	783	1 015	29.6	1 072	1 325	23.6
Finland	478	314	−34.3	731	803	9.8	906	1 201	32.6
Norway	208	162	−22.1	558	568	1.8	731	1 182	61.7
Ireland	283	209	−26.1	312	371	18.9	450	561	24.7
Luxembourg	13	9	−30.8	61	60	−1.6	65	90	38.5
Iceland	15	13	−13.3	30	40	33.3	36	52	44.4
Total OECD	40 126	32 332	−19.4	107 420	109 589	2.0	143 417	183 768	28.1

1.   Ranked by civilian employment in services in 1980.
2.   Including hunting, forestry and fishing.
3.   Major divisions 2, 3, 4, and 5 of the I.S.I.C.
4.   Major divisions 6, 7, 8, 9 and 0 of the I.S.I.C.
Source :   OECD.

26

1980, counterbalanced by a reduction in the primary sector from 30 per cent to 10 per cent in the same period. This trend is continuing, particularly under government encouragement to science and technology. RD spending is 2.4 per cent of GNP, the same as the United States but with a negligible military component. In Japan one-third of investment in manufacturing in 1985 was in the "high tech" area.

The urban policy implications of these economic trends are that:

   i)   Industrial land in cities is becoming available for redevelopment;
   ii) New industrial development is moving to suburban locations;
   iii) Increasing pressure is put on central area sites, particularly office space in Tokyo;
   iv) There is a chance to use developing sectors of the economy to steer related growth, as for example through the 18 "technopolis" schemes considered in the next chapter; and
   v)   There is a decline in urban areas heavily dependent on traditional manufacturing, particularly receiving government assistance under the Urgent Measures for Stabilization of Specified Industries Act, 1978.

Three further points of relevance to urban policy arise, related to the above trends.

First, the growth of services is likely to favour female employment, which could lead to further decentralisation in larger cities, as employment locations nearer residential areas become more convenient. This would reinforce the decongestion trend referred to earlier, as new manufacturing industries seek suburban locations. Related to a point made earlier, about the size of the public sector, prefectural administrative capitals, such as Fukuoka, have shown a recent tendency to grow (Table 8) and this would be reinforced by decentralisation of powers and a growth in the public sector generally. While not a large increase, the share of employment in central and local government rose from 3.3 per cent to 3.6 per cent between 1970 and 1980.

Secondly, the restructuring of the Japanese economy, as elsewhere in OECD, is generally favouring the establishment of small enterprises, although increasing competition in the retail and wholesale sectors could lead to a considerable overall reduction in the number of small enterprises. Already the Japanese economy contains a high proportion of small firms. 58 per cent of the workforce is in firms under 30 as opposed, for example, to 25 per cent in the United States. The average size of firm in Japan is 15 people, as opposed to 30 in the United States. This trend reinforces urban policy flexibility. Although they often need specialised skills, small firms do not need large labour markets, and can choose small town locations. Another effect is to reduce the role of government in industrial development, which has tended to be well developed in Japan in respect of the large conglomerate firms.

The third industrial trend, which will have a significant effect on the demand for urban services, is the fall in the length of the working week. Between 1970 and 1980 the proportion of people working a 6 day week fell from approximately three-quarters to a quarter. This has been accompanied by a growth in the length of holidays and shorter working hours. It can be expected that more time will be spent in towns for recreational rather than work purposes. Demands on sports facilities and parks are likely to increase significantly as a result.

There is a clear cut need to achieve harmonization between urban and economic policies. This is particularly so in the field of industrial policy as the distribution of economic activity influences the location of urban development and the chances of achieving urban revitalisation. In the last two decades, economic and urban policies were not always in harmony. However, there are increasing signs that the two types of policy are converging, the technopolis projects quoted later are an example.

27

Table 8. **Prefectural capitals population growth, 1970-1980**

Prefecture	[1]	Capital	1970[2]	1975[3]	1980	Total change 1970-1980 %
Chiba	12	Chiba	365 389	528 174	634 732	73.7
Shiga	25	Otsu	93 374	124 637	159 678	71.0
Nara	29	Nara	144 205	181 762	245 546	70.3
Oita	44	Oita	134 849	174 836	228 204	69.2
Ehime	38	Matsuyama	182 808	239 386	297 104	62.5
Miyazaki	45	Miyazaki	116 261	137 401	183 566	57.9
Saitama	11	Urawa	213 842	287 749	330 224	54.4
Hokkaido	1	Sapporo	823 233	1 038 647	1 265 054	53.7
Ibaraki	8	Mito	92 182	116 833	140 175	52.1
Gumma	10	Maebashi	121 457	151 115	181 444	49.4
Fukushima	7	Fukushima	96 016	118 762	137 617	43.3
Niigata	15	Niigata	275 780	338 027	394 689	43.1
Okayama	33	Okayama	218 735	247 957	308 594	41.1
Aomori	2	Aomori	162 542	199 405	226 801	39.5
Akita	5	Akita	156 002	188 836	217 056	39.1
Fukuoka	40	Fukuoka	720 202	859 430	999 477	38.8
Tochigi	9	Utsunomiya	187 958	223 471	257 955	37.2
Kagoshima	46	Kagoshima	306 508	353 233	419 775	37.0
Iwate	3	Morioka	144 280	167 920	196 494	36.2
Kanagawa	14	Yokohama	1 935 401	2 385 241	2 594 398	34.0
Miyagi	4	Sendai	439 290	532 460	584 140	33.0
Kochi	39	Kochi	180 658	206 836	237 361	31.4
Nagano	20	Nagano	135 982	145 068	177 331	30.4
Shimane	32	Matsue	67 711	71 578	87 541	29.3
Saga	41	Saga	84 903	881 165	109 660	29.2
Yamagata	6	Yamagata	115 907	125 432	149 156	28.7
Hiroshima	34	Hiroshima	579 082	678 407	740 899	27.9
Shizuoka	22	Shizuoka	292 732	347 479	373 096	27.5
Ishikawa	17	Kanazawa	251 185	273 177	317 983	26.6
Fukui	18	Fukui	115 881	132 534	142 169	22.7
Kumamoto	43	Kumamoto	346 885	379 589	425 558	22.7
Toyama	16	Toyama	151 928	160 629	184 872	21.7
Tokushima	36	Tokushima	141 343	154 631	170 156	20.4
Kagawa	37	Takamatsu	170 937	179 426	204 433	19.6
Yamanashi	19	Kofu	136 217	142 726	159 544	17.1
Tottori	31	Tottori	59 261	67 121	68 562	15.7
Okinawa	47	Naha	253 057	276 708	290 625	14.8
Mie	24	Tsu	80 086	89 918	91 467	14.2
Wakayama	30	Wakayama	253 993	277 522	286 615	12.8
Yamaguchi	35	Yamaguchi	39 393	39 855	44 173	12.1
Nagasaki	42	Nagasaki	314 458	336 025	345 980	10.0
Aichi	23	Nagoya	1 854 273	1 949 388	2 001 908	8.0
Hyogo	28	Kobe	1 155 727	1 226 133	1 240 452	7.3
Gifu	21	Gifu	263 910	285 071	280 574	6.3
Kyoto	26	Kyoto	1 301 277	1 363 411	1 373 395	5.5
Tokyo	13	Tokyo	8 793 123	8 643 033	8 351 893	−5.0
Osaka	27	Osaka	2 977 661	2 778 268	2 647 484	−11.1

1. Prefectural code number. Prefectures are ranked by percentage changes in population between 1970 and 1980.
2. Figures refer to population within city boundaries as defined at October 1975.
3. Figures refer to population within city boundaries as defined at October 1980.
Source: Population Census of Japan, Special Volume, Densely Inhabited Districts, 1975 and 1980 editions.

C. The Agricultural Sector

Urban policies are concerned with the spatial arrangement of social and economic activities: land availability is, therefore, a vital consideration. Because the agricultural industry is a major user of land, there is a close interaction between agricultural policies and urban policies. The area of arable land has fallen by approximately one-tenth, from 6.0 million to 5.4 million hectares in the past 20 years. However, in contrast to many other

28

OECD countries, the major policy concern in Japan is not the loss of good agricultural land for urban development, but the constraints on development posed by the nature of agricultural land holding in urban areas.

In the recent measures that have been taken to make the Japanese economy more open, the agricultural industry has remained relatively privileged. Although the value of food imports into Japan is the highest in the world, at 1.1 per cent of GNP they are in the same range as Germany (1.2 per cent) and the United Kingdom (1.4 per cent). Despite the support for the agricultural sector, the decline of primary sector employment, referred to earlier, is strongly influenced by changes in agricultural employment. The number of households employed full time in agriculture fell by half, from approximately 1.2 million to 0.6 million between 1965 and 1985. Total employment in agriculture declined by approximately one-third to 8 per cent in the same period.

However, the average size of holding has only risen from just under to just over 1 hectare. Although tastes are becoming more diverse and subsidies are available for other grain crops, the high level of subsidy available for rice production seems to be one of the factors which encourages households to cultivate small holdings on a part-time basis. 68 per cent of families involved in farming in Japan do so on a part-time basis to supplement the main source of family income from employment in manufacturing. Expectations of capital gains from increases in the price of land have reinforced the reluctance to sell. Numerous small agricultural land parcels in urban areas make the achievement of a rational pattern of residential development difficult and, while contributing to the area of green open space, the land is not available for recreation in the same sense as an urban park.

Although it is not the role of this report to review agricultural policies in Japan, a continued high level of support for agricultural production seems to be one of the factors which encourages the maintenance of small agricultural land holdings in urban areas. These represent a limit to achieving the urban policy objectives the government has set. One factor which points to a possible change in this situation is the high average age of farming households and the next generation of urban Japanese are probably unlikely to maintain a part-time family involvement in farming. In this light agricultural policy in Japan will need to be re-examined and more closely integrated with urban policy, if the urbanisation trends for the rest of this century are to be successfully handled.

D. Administrative Framework

There are several Japanese ministries and agencies with direct responsibilities for urban policies. The Ministry of Construction (MOC) has a direct interest in town planning legislation, the financing and provision of housing and infrastructure, urban renewal and land readjustment projects, parks and green spaces, and highway planning, sewerage provision and flood control. The titles of the five main Bureaux – Economic, City, River, Road and Housing – indicate the range covered. MOC has an important outreach into prefectural and municipal affairs through direct contacts and the secondment of staff. It also has an extensive network of local offices. MOC's involvement in policy implementation is via an interlocking system of five year plans for Flood Control, Road Development, Sewerage System, Urban Parks Development, Traffic Safety Facilities, House Construction and Steep Slope Failure Prevention Works.

Besides the MOC, the Prime Minister's Office has a potentially influential role to play in policy making through its responsibilities for the National Land Agency (NLA). The powers available are essentially those of the coordination of others, based on the National Land Use

Map 3

PREFECTURES IN JAPAN

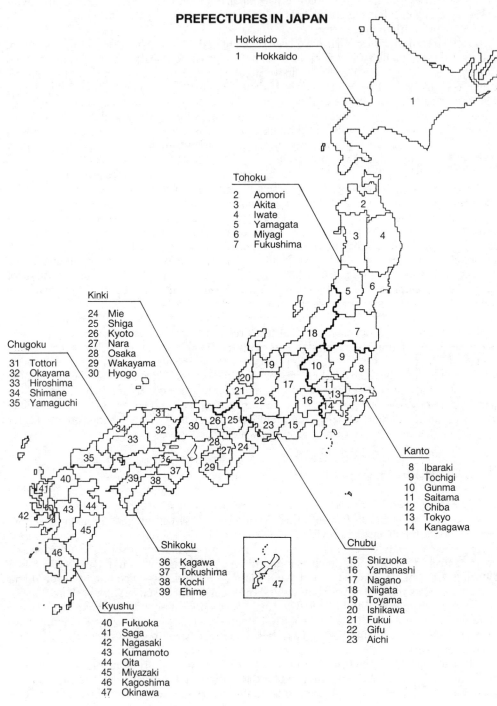

Hokkaido
1   Hokkaido

Tohoku
2   Aomori
3   Akita
4   Iwate
5   Yamagata
6   Miyagi
7   Fukushima

Kinki
24   Mie
25   Shiga
26   Kyoto
27   Nara
28   Osaka
29   Wakayama
30   Hyogo

Chugoku
31   Tottori
32   Okayama
33   Hiroshima
34   Shimane
35   Yamaguchi

Kanto
8   Ibaraki
9   Tochigi
10   Gunma
11   Saitama
12   Chiba
13   Tokyo
14   Kanagawa

Shikoku
36   Kagawa
37   Tokushima
38   Kochi
39   Ehime

Chubu
15   Shizuoka
16   Yamanashi
17   Nagano
18   Niigata
19   Toyama
20   Ishikawa
21   Fukui
22   Gifu
23   Aichi

Kyushu
40   Fukuoka
41   Saga
42   Nagasaki
43   Kumamoto
44   Oita
45   Miyazaki
46   Kagoshima
47   Okinawa

Acts, but the Land Price Publication Act (Chapter 4) is also administered by the NLA. As will also be seen from later chapters the Ministry of Transport and the Ministry of Home Affairs, responsible for local government finance and administration, have significant roles to play which influence urban policy. The Ministry of International Trade and Industry, Ministry of Agriculture, Forestry and Fisheries and the NLA also can exert important, though partial, influences on urban policy.

Although the major focus of this report is on the urban policy of central government, implementation is very much dependent on local government. Japan has two levels of local government – prefectures and municipalities – with functions set out in the Local Autonomy Act, 1947. The functions of local government in the Act cover generally the maintenance of public order, safety, health and welfare of inhabitants and visitors. Detailed responsibilities cover public open space, water courses, service networks, transport installations and educational, cultural and health facilities. In addition, labour relations, industrial promotion and consumer protection functions are mentioned in the Local Autonomy Act. More closely related to urban policy, local authorities in Japan have responsibility for land management and development; historical and cultural conservation; building and zoning regulations; and city planning and land readjustment (Chapter 4).

In essence the municipalities have the prime responsibilities for all local government functions, with the Prefectures only having powers where a wider approach is required to parts of these functions (e.g. water management); where inter-municipality co-operation may be required (e.g. city planning); and where a certain scale of support for a service is necessary (e.g. major infrastructure provision). The respective responsibilities of municipalities and Prefectures are set out in the specific legislation on the topic concerned.

However, Prefectural Governors have another range of functions which are in the form of powers delegated from central government. In respect of these functions the Prefectural Governor, although elected at large, is responsible to the national government. However, the real limit to local government action is not legal powers, but the financial reliance on Central Government and in particular the Ministry of Home Affairs. The discussion of local government finance is developed later (Chapter 7).

Japan's governmental system at prefectural and municipal level reflects a hierarchy with respective powers which are well defined and mutually understood. There is a reasonable relationship between the functions and the boundaries of the regional and local units of administration, and this gives Japan a sound basis for constructing and maintaining a coherent urban development system and for implementing urban policies. There has been a progressive reduction of local government units in Japan from over 10 000 in the early 1950s to 3 255 in 1980. However, there has been stability at the prefectural level, where the 47 prefectures were established in 1889 (Map 3). An exception to this general structure is the case of "designated" cities, which have additional powers and considerable political and financial influence which they can exercise through direct links with central government[6].

The growth of the public sector generally and of local spending in particular has given increasing powers to the local level, particularly as many prefectural powers are often delegated to municipalities. However, this devolution of authority is counteracted by two other features of Japanese administration. First, there are more than 100 public corporations. Secondly, besides these national public corporations, there are 3 000 local public corporations, many responsible for land development, housing and infrastructure provision[7].

These public corporations are a feature of urban policy implementation in Japan which is of particular interest to other OECD countries. Established by statute, the objectives of these corporations are to achieve particular tasks in ways more akin to the private sector than local government. They are particularly active in the execution of urban development projects.

E. Policy Conclusions

To be effective, urban policy needs to be integrated with a range of other policies. In the economic field a sustained rate of growth, combined with low inflation and low interest rates, provides a platform for increased expenditure on the implementation of urban policy. Public debt levels are comparatively high, but the high savings ratio and the prospect of continued economic growth suggest that more private investment will be available to support the expansion of domestic demand.

In particular, industrial policy needs to be closely allied to urban policy. Two important changes are taking place in the structure of Japanese industry. As in other comparable OECD countries the service sector is growing, but not at the expense of manufacturing which is maintaining its role. The primary sector is in decline but is still large and further contraction can be anticipated, particularly if agriculture becomes more efficient. The agricultural sector is itself one that has significant interactions with urban development. Both agricultural and urban policies have an interest in land resources, especially in and near the large metropolitan areas.

Another important trend, which is gaining momentum, will also affect future urban development. Policies towards the growth of leisure time, linked to the ageing of the population considered in the next chapter, will greatly influence the demands on certain types of urban facilities and services, particularly for recreation. These trends are likely to lead to more people spending more of their time in or near their homes. This will put a higher premium on the quality both of housing and of the neighbourhood environment. These concerns will need to be reflected in future urban policy priorities.

Urban policy making in Japan is becoming more complex. Increasing attention needs to be given to patterns of metropolitan migration, urban renovation and quality objectives, particularly in housing. These issues have been added to the more familiar list of concerns – national migration patterns, new urban development and quantitative aims, for example for infrastructure provision. It is not the purpose of this Report to investigate public administration in Japan, but a reassessment of policies often implies a review of policy institutions. In outline, what is required is one focus for urban policy formulation and implementation at national level and a new mechanism to ensure that urban policies and other related policies are evolved in harmony.

At the same time, to cope successfully with a more complex urban situation, more diversity of policy response will be required. This implies an active role for local government, with central government concentrating on achieving its own objectives and ensuring that local governments are provided with the necessary capability. The overall situation described in this chapter is one in which, rather than excessive central control, there is fragmentation of policy formulation and implementation. Also at the central level policy making co-ordination is not apparent.

For urban policies in Japan to improve their effectiveness in securing the objectives that have been set, a major initiative will need to be made to ensure that urban policy and other major policy areas are developed in unison. Utilising existing institutions, the National Land Agency is well placed to be developed into the forum for the co-ordination of urban policy with other central government policies. However, close links would be needed between the Agency and the Ministry of Construction with its responsibility for the initial formulation and eventual implementation of urban policy.

NOTES AND REFERENCES

1. *Economic Surveys 1984/1985*, OECD, Paris, 1985 and *Economic Outlook* No. 37, OECD, Paris, 1985.

2. A Japanese Viewpoint, Dr. S. Okita, *OECD Observer* No. 127, Paris, 1984.

3. Diet ordered to redraw electoral boundaries, *Financial Times*, 18.7.85.

4. The Role of the Public Sector, *OECD Economic Studies* No. 4, OECD, Paris, 1985.

5. Maturing of the Japanese Economy in the 1980s, *National Westminster Bank Quarterly Review*, November, 1983.

6. The 10 designated cities are Osaka, Nagoya, Kyoto, Yokohama, Kobe, Kitakyushu, Kawasaki, Fukuoka, Sapporo and Hiroshima. They have city planning, land adjustment, building standards and a wide range of other powers similar to the Prefectures.

7. *The Politics of Regional Policy in Japan*, R. J. Samuels, Princeton University Press, 1985.

Chapter 3

BALANCED DEVELOPMENT

The scale and agglomeration economies represented by cities in general and the particular locational advantages of individual cities are the main factors which act together to concentrate urban development. In most countries a dominant city emerges as can be illustrated for the OECD countries (Table 9). However, in Japan this process has been developed to a high degree, considering also the close geographical proximity of the three largest metropolitan areas, grouped in a 400 km arc along the south Pacific coast.

Table 9. **Primate cities in OECD countries, 1980[1]**

Thousands and Percentage

Countries[2]	Population in major urban areas		Major urban areas' share of total population (%)	
	Largest	3 largest	Largest	3 largest
Iceland	118	142	51.4	61.9
Canada	2 975	7 033	23.6	55.9
Luxembourg	107	163	29.4	45.0
Australia	2 875	6 396	19.7	43.9
New Zealand	770	1 381	24.2	43.5
Denmark	1 746	2 066	34.1	40.3
Greece	3 027	3 880	31.1	39.8
Austria	1 961	2 668	25.9	35.3
Portugal	2 257	3 457	23.0	35.2
Ireland	984	1 183	29.2	35.1
Japan	23 629	37 697	20.2	32.2
Sweden	1 386	2 534	16.7	30.5
Norway	821	1 212	20.1	29.6
Belgium	1 009	2 492	10.2	25.3
Switzerland	837	1 569	13.2	24.7
United Kingdom	6 713	11 958	12.0	21.4
France	8 707	11 039	16.0	20.3
Netherlands	1 016	2 647	7.2	18.8
Finland	759	874	15.9	18.3
Turkey	4 657	8 176	10.4	18.3
Italy	3 295	8 853	5.8	15.6
Spain	3 188	5 694	8.4	15.1
Germany	4 814	9 225	7.8	15.0
United States	9 120	23 700	4.0	10.5
Total OECD	86 771	156 040	11.3	20.3

1. Or nearest available year.
2. Countries ranked by percentage share of total population in the three largest urban areas.
Source: OECD, National Yearbooks and Statistical Yearbooks.

When carried to a certain level, depending on economic and social circumstances, the process of urban concentration produces negative externalities in the form of congestion, pollution and inflation. Many OECD governments have, therefore, sought to assist the process of achieving a more balanced national distribution of urban development. Among the particular urban policy concerns voiced in Japan have been increased natural disaster risks, high land prices, solid and water waste disposal problems, access difficulties, noise nuisance and long commuting distances.

A. Urban Population Trends

In the first chapter the high level and rapid rate of growth of the Japanese urban population are highlighted. Another remarkable feature is, however, the extent to which this growth, until very recently, was concentrated in the three metropolitan areas. In those terms the national policies to limit the growth of Tokaido were not successful in the 1960s and 1970s. The changing balance between migration and natural increase is a further interesting aspect of metropolitan growth trends (Table 10).

Table 10. **Natural increase and migration in metropolitan Japan, 1955-1980**

Thousands

		National capital	Kinki	Chubu	National total
	Total	2 329	1 217	564	4 245
1955-60	Natural Increase	1 172	700	706	–
	Migration	1 157	517	–142	–
	Total	3 178	1 771	825	4 908
1960-65	Natural Increase	1 538	954	794	–
	Migration	1 640	818	31	–
	Total	3 295	1 647	907	5 456
1965-70	Natural Increase	1 999	1 183	910	–
	Migration	1 295	464	–4	–
	Total	3 364	1 542	1 242	7 274
1970-75	Natural Increase	2 382	1 395	1 128	–
	Migration	981	147	114	–
	Total	2 080	272	853	5 121
1975-80	Natural Increase	1 657	981	864	–
	Migration	321	–209	–11	–

Source: Ministry of Construction.

Migration levels in Japan reached their peak around 1970 (Table 11)[1]. The Tokyo metropolitan area, for example, was gaining 260 000 migrants annually between 1965 and 1970, a rate that had fallen to 65 000 p.a. 10 years later. Since 1981 the annual rate has been rising again and, in 1983, rose to 109 000. The three large metropolitan areas gained a total population of 1.2 M p.a. in the 1960s, a rate that had fallen to 0.93M p.a. in the early 1970s. Also after 1975 small towns of under 50 000 which had been losing population before that date started to gain.

35

Table 11. **Population migration 1955-1983**

Thousands

Year	Total	Intra-prefectural	Inter-prefectural
1955	5 141	2 914	2 227
1960	5 653	2 973	2 680
1965	7 380	3 688	3 692
1970	8 273	4 038	4 235
1975	7 544	3 846	3 698
1980	7 067	3 711	3 356
1983	6 674	3 478	3 196

Source: Ministry of Construction.

The resulting population densities of 14 000+ per km^2 in Tokyo are extremely high by any standards, and compare to the 322 per km^2 average for Japan. In comparison with the London and Paris regions with 18 per cent of their respective national populations, the Tokyo region has 30 per cent. The migration levels are declining and changing their nature as the agricultural sector moves towards equilibrium and land prices and congestion discourage those who might move to the larger cities. Two typical migration patterns have emerged, typified as the "U-turn" and the "J-turn". The former consists of migration from a rural area to a large city, followed by a return to a rural area[2].

The J-turn by which migrants move to a large city from a rural area, often for higher education, and then move to a smaller urban area to find employment and higher standards of environment is the most convincing analysis of the new pattern. However, the general importance of migration has declined and it is natural increase which will boost the metropolitan area population in future[3]. Within the general pattern of metropolitan growth certain central parts of the large cities have been losing population, the so-called "doughnut" phenomenon. Central Tokyo was declining by 1960, followed by Osaka and Nagoya in the early and late sixties respectively.

Another aspect of balance is commuting to central Tokyo (Diagram 2). In 1980 Chiyoda-ku, a central ward of Tokyo, had a daytime population of 937 000 and a night-time population of 55 000, a ratio of 17 to 1. Only 17 of the 161 cities in the national capital region have a daytime residential ratio of more than one and all 17 have populations below 200 000. Other measures of centralisation serve to reinforce the impression given by the population figures. Of the head offices listed on the Tokyo Stock Exchange in 1975, approximately 55 per cent were in the National Capital Region, 25 per cent in Kinki and 6 per cent in Chubu. Three-quarters of university students were being educated in the same three metropolitan regions in 1975.

Another specific demographic feature which will affect urban policies in Japan is the ageing of the population (Diagram 3). Japan still has a young population profile, with 9 per cent of the population over 65 against 11 per cent in the United States, 14 per cent in France and 15 per cent in Germany. But the Japanese population profile is now ageing at a speed unparalleled in the OECD. The proportion of over-65s will have risen from 5 to 12 per cent in the 45 years from 1950 to 1995, whereas the same rise took 175 years in France and 80 years in Germany. At 15.6 per cent in the year 2000, the proportion of over-65s will have either reached or exceeded that of other OECD countries. This ageing of the population will change

36

Diagram 2

COMMUTING TO CENTRAL TOKYO, 1975-1980

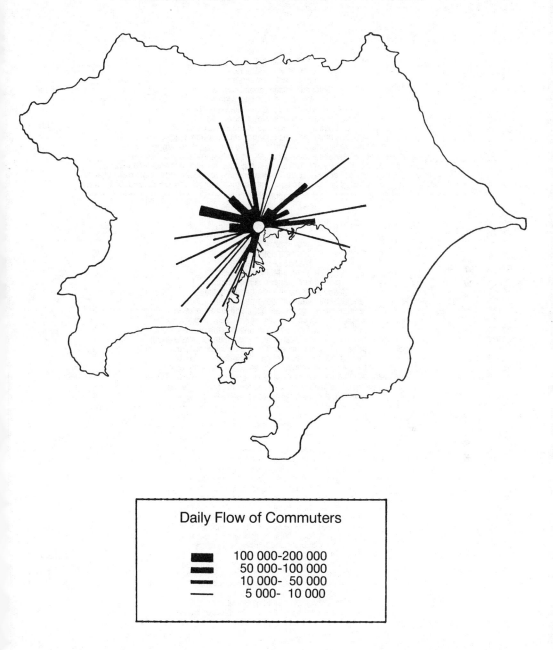

Daily Flow of Commuters

- 100 000-200 000
- 50 000-100 000
- 10 000- 50 000
- 5 000- 10 000

Source :   *Tokyo Region Person Trip Survey*

Diagram 3

AGEING OF THE JAPANESE POPULATION, 1920-2025

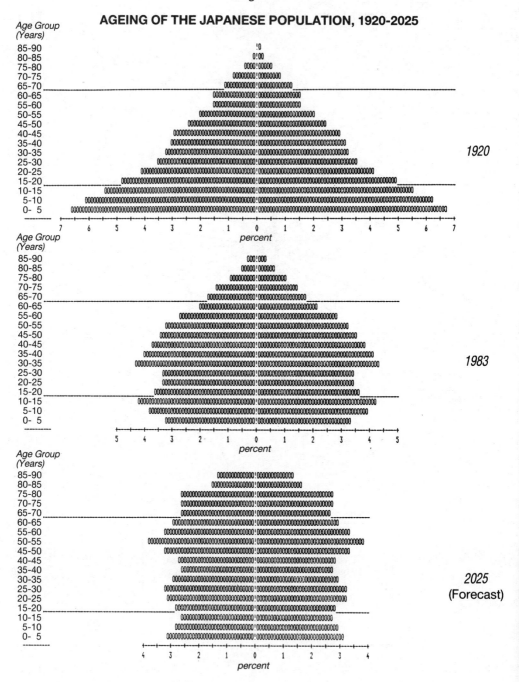

Source: *Japan Statistical Yearbook 1984, Institute of Population Problems, Ministry of Health and Welfare, Japan.*

the pattern of demand for urban services, reinforcing the needs for increased social capital expenditure.

B.   National Urban Policy

The population pre-eminence of Tokyo goes back several centuries, but the roots of its recent growth can be traced back to the period of rapid industrialisation in the last sixty years. In 1929 it is estimated that 17 per cent of the value of industrial output was produced in Tokyo. Taking into account the development of Tokyo from a city into a metropolis, it is now estimated that one-third of Japan's wealth is generated in the Tokyo metropolitan area. The last 40 years have seen a series of plans and other measures both to avoid the further concentration of population and employment in the three major, contiguous metropolitan areas collectively known as Tokaido – National Capital (based on Tokyo), Kinki (based on Osaka) and Chubu (based on Nagoya) – and also to structure the development of these three metropolitan areas[4]. Nevertheless, throughout the period the major industrial and infrastructure investment continued to be in Tokaido.

Decentralisation policies were first considered, as in some European countries, in the early 1940s, based on reasons of national security. However, the main thrust of policies with balanced national development as their objective can be traced to the Comprehensive National Land Development Act, 1950. Even so it was not until 1962 that the first National Comprehensive Development Plan was approved, based on the concept of establishing growth poles outside the major metropolitan areas. In the interim three principally economic plans with national growth objectives formed the basis of policy (1955, 1957, 1960). The last of these was dubbed the "doubling national income plan", which concentrated investment in the Pacific industrial belt.

By 1962 the industrial economy of Japan, based on the three major metropolitan areas, was already in a period of rapid growth. In retrospect it can be seen that the opportunity to establish policies and programmes for balanced development passed by default in the dozen years between the passing of the Act and the publication of the first Plan. In this period heavy investment in private industry, backed by central government economic and industrial policies, took place in Tokaido contradicting the aims of the 1950 Act.

Nevertheless, the first National Comprehensive Development Plan adopted a "growth pole" strategy. Under the New Industrial Towns Development Act, 1962, and the Industrial Development of Special Areas Act, 1964, 15 new industrial cities together with six special areas for industrial development were designated (Map 4). A study of these new cities shows that these initiatives were generally successful, but clearly the amount of development attracted to the designated areas did little to stem the tide of migration to Tokaido[5].

The second National Comprehensive Development Plan was published in 1969. While the accent was still on economic development, environmental and welfare objectives were introduced. The Plan had four themes – the effective utilisation of land; promotion of local development; the preservation and enhancement of amenities; and a balance between the man-made and natural environments. The growth poles concept linked to restraints in the three metropolitan areas was continued. Legislative support for further decentralisation followed in the form of the Promotion of Industrial Relocation Act, 1972.

In the 1969 Plan emphasis was placed on large-scale development projects and improved communications. However, the construction of the Shinkansen railway system, linking Tokyo and Osaka in 1964, and the national motorway system had probably done more to consolidate Tokaido than any other public investments. The extension of the Shinkansen to Fukuoka in

Map 4

NEW TOWNS AND SPECIAL INDUSTRIAL DEVELOPMENT AREAS IN JAPAN

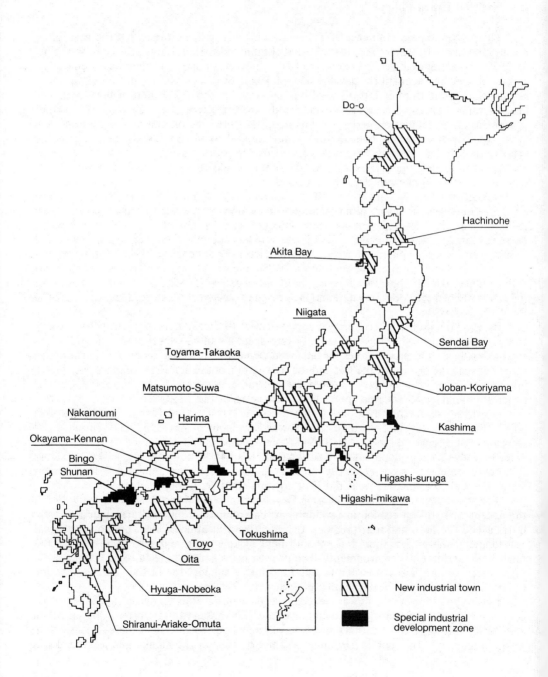

1975 merely extended the existing intensely developed urban crescent, and only contributed to more balanced development to a limited extent. Nine of the ten Japanese cities of over 1 million population were then linked by Shinkansen.

The National Land Use Planning Act, 1974, considerably extended the scope of its 1950 predecessor and developed the concept of a long-term national land use plan. Concerns with finding locations for development were replaced by the objective of managing and conserving land as a limited resource. A National Land Use Plan was required in addition to the Comprehensive National Land Development Plan of the 1950 Act and more emphasis was put on prefectural and municipal plans.

Although the 1970s saw four further economic plans (1970, 1973, 1976 and 1979), beginning to reflect the environmental concerns arising from rapid and largely unregulated urban development, there was an eight year gap between the second and the third National Comprehensive Development Plan (Sanzenso), which was approved in 1977. The changing pattern of urbanisation, with inter-prefectural migration rates declining, was reflected by the third plan's concept of "Teijyu-ken" (settling down in a certain area). The stress was put on developing provincial cities as a way of stabilising the Japanese urban system. The plan, based on stimulating local economic development, was running in the same direction as social and economic trends. Income differentials in the period 1970-80 also narrowed, the difference between the richest and poorest prefectures falling from 43 to 26 points on a scale with 100 as the average national figure (1970 range 124-81, 1980 range 114-88). The third National Comprehensive Development Plan of 1977 has run for a nine year period and a fourth Plan is now in draft.

C. Metropolitan Balance

Besides the national perspective on balanced development, the three principal metro-politan areas have been the subject of legislative and planning action in their own right, also starting in 1950. As with the National Planning measures to achieve a greater degree of developmental equilibrium at the national scale, there has not been either the public support or political will to restructure the metropolitan areas in a more balanced way. The Capital City Construction Act, 1950, as was to be expected at the time, concentrated on major projects such as Haneda airport, improving the port and underground railway facilities, and new amenities such as Yoyogi Park. The National Capital Region Development Act of 1956, and similar albeit belated legislation for Kinki and Chubu following in 1963 and 1966 respectively, were the basis for more considered attempts to structure urban growth.

Under the Consolidation of the Urban Development Area of the National Capital Region Act, 1958, the first plan for the Tokyo Metropolitan Area was published. It comprised a basic scheme for 17 years, a more detailed consolidation plan and a project plan, which was linked to expenditure in individual financial years. A classical approach was adopted with three types of designation: the Existing Urban Zone; the Suburban Zone; and the City Development Zone. Influenced by the Abercrombie Plan for the London Region[6], 18 city development zones were proposed as sites for satellite towns, as well as a 10 km wide green belt. Legislation was also passed on the control of industrial location. In 1959, following the publication of the Plan, the Restriction of Industry and other Similar Functions in Existing Urban Areas of the National Capital Region Act was adopted. This act restricted the construction of factories and universities, the concentration of the latter being particularly pronounced in Tokyo. The projections for 1975 of the population within 100 km of Tokyo were revised upwards from 26.6 million to 28.2 million.

In the second plan for the Tokyo metropolitan area, formulated in 1968 ten years after the first, the 1975 forecast for the National Capital Region was further revised upwards to 33.1 million. The Green Belt proposal in the first plan was abandoned following pressure from landowners. The Promotion of Industrial Relocation Act, 1972, was a further attempt to restructure the metropolitan areas. To supplement the provisions of the 1962 and 1964 Acts, "relocation promotion areas" and "inducement areas" were designated offering a range of tax benefits, subsidies and loans. Industrial parks were also established in the Suburban and City Development Zones of two metropolitan areas. By 1985 26 industrial parks had been established in the National Capital region and four in Kinki.

One of the reasons given for the failure to develop new areas in a comprehensive and planned way was reluctance on behalf of the local authorities concerned. In the mid-1960s and again in the mid-1970s legislation aimed at overcoming this opposition was passed. The first legislation, the Special Measures pertaining to the Financing of the State for Development of the Suburban Consolidation Zone and Similar Places in the National Capital Region and Kinki Act, 1966, authorised the raising of bond issue ceilings and the percentage of central government finance for infrastructure. This was followed in 1970 by similar legislation for Chubu. The second measure was the Workshop Tax, introduced in 1975, allowing local authorities to raise money for "consolidation measures" based on the profits of companies operating in their area .

The current plan for the Tokyo Metropolitan Area, adopted in 1976, is based on six objectives:

i)   Developing the political, economic and cultural role;
ii) Strict control of the concentration of population and industry in the Existing Urban Zone and the Suburban Development Zone;
iii) Consolidating the multicentred nature of the metropolitan area;
iv) Augmenting social and cultural facilities, as well as transport, in the main cities;
v)   Maintaining an affluent and "comfortable" metropolitan community; and
vi) Promoting the rational use of land and the preservation of environmental standards.

As in Japanese plans at the national level, a classical approach can be noted with three zones identified: the Existing Urban Zone; the Suburban Development Zone; and the City Development Zone. However, the plan is now ten years old and office employment has continued to concentrate in central Tokyo. Similar approaches have been adopted in Kinki and Chubu, where the latest metropolitan plans both date from 1978. The same types of zoning reappear, as do similar general objectives, including an increased stress on environmental standards.

Current thinking about the plan for the city of Tokyo is based on an attempt to restructure the conurbation as a multi-core city. The existence of a single core is criticised for the long commuting distances, the disorderly development and the depopulation of the centre, as commercial uses displace housing. Hachioji, Tachikawa, Machida and Tama have been selected as centres in the metropolitan area, while in the 23 ward area, Shinjuku, Shibuya, Ikebukuro, Ueno, Asakusa, Kinshicho, Kameido and Osaki are suggested as sub-centres within Tokyo itself.

D.   New Towns

New towns have played an important role in Japanese urban policy. The New Towns Development Corporation was not formed until 1975, well after the major growth pole

Table 12. **Major Japanese new towns**

New town	Prefecture	Project period	Planned population
Tama	Tokyo	1966-90	373 000
Chiba	Chiba	1969-93	340 000
Kohoku	Kanagawa	1974-92	300 000
Ichihara	Chiba	1977-92	130 000
Hokusetsu	Hyogo	1971-93	100 000
Hokushin	Hyogo	1966-93	89 000
Tsukuba	Ibaraki	1968-85	100 000
Kozoji	Aichi	1977-92	81 000
Ryugasaki	Ibaraki	1977-92	75 000
Heijo	Kyoto	1965-90	73 000
Total			1 661 000

Source: Ministry of Construction.

proposals, at the national and metropolitan level, had been formulated. But before that date the Japan Housing Corporation had been responsible for 27 new towns[7]. The New Towns Development Corporation only had a life of six years, being brought together with the Japan Housing Corporation to form the Japan Housing and Urban Development Corporation (JHUDC) in 1981. However, the JHUDC is still active with several new towns in its current programme (Table 12). The Japan Regional Development Corporation, established in 1974, also has a new towns programme, but on a smaller scale and with regional as opposed to urban policy objectives.

One particular new town has received international attention. At Tsukuba, 60 km north-east of Tokyo, a concerted effort has been made to decentralise government research institutes from central Tokyo. Starting from the Tsukuba Academic City Construction Act, 1970, 45 government and three private research institutes have been relocated. Difficulty has been experienced in attracting research workers at the Institutes and their families to live in Tsukuba, because of the lack of social facilities. The eventual population of 220 000 (100 000 in the new town) has not been realised and at the present time the population of the area stands at 142 000 (October 1984). However, as the town matures and as the workforce comes to consist of new recruits, rather than staff from Tokyo, barriers to movement should diminish. The interest of Tsukuba is to illustrate what can be achieved with the existing Japanese system. Experience has been gained on decentralising the tertiary sector to add to earlier experiences with industrial decentralisation. Tsukuba also represents the close links that are being developed between science and technology policies and urban policy. Experience at Tsukuba laid the foundation for the latest legislation to promote development in non-metropolitan Japan.

The next phase of new towns policies is represented by the Promotion of Regional Development for High Technology Industrial Complexes Act, 1983, the so-called "Technopolis Act". This has led to the designation of 18 sites, by the end of 1985 (Map 5). Kumamoto on the "Silicon Island" of Kyushu was one of the first to be designated under criteria based on:

i) Being away from areas where industry is heavily concentrated;

ii) Suitability for industrial development from the physical, economic and social perspectives;

Map 5

TECHNOPOLIS LOCATIONS

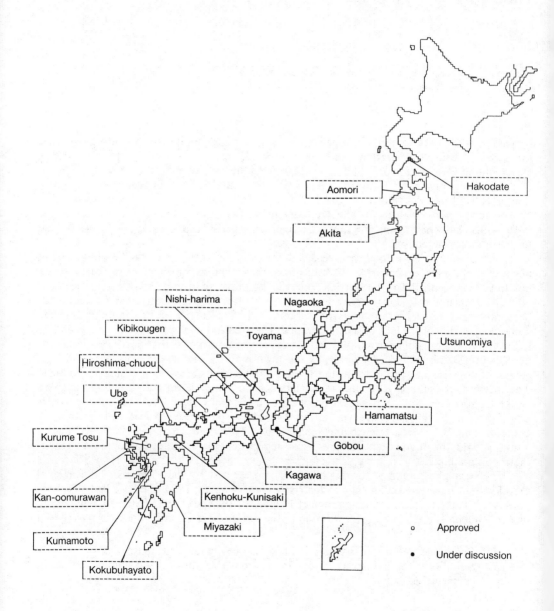

Aomori

Hakodate

Akita

Nishi-harima

Nagaoka

Kibikougen

Toyama

Utsunomiya

Hiroshima-chuou

Ube

Hamamatsu

Kurume Tosu

Gobou

Kagawa

Kan-oomurawan

Kenhoku-Kunisaki

Miyazaki

Kumamoto

Kokubuhayato

○   Approved

●   Under discussion

iii) Existence of a certain number of companies with potential for either the development or application of high technology;
iv) Availability of land for industrial development, water and other services;
v) In or near a city with 150 000+ population;
vi) Presence of a university where high technology is a subject of study; and
vii) Easy access to high speed transportation facilities.

The technopolises combine national economic and industrial development policy objectives with urban policy objectives. Soft loans, local tax exemptions and 30 per cent depreciation allowance for industrial assets are available to private firms. An important thrust of the proposals is to engage the prefectures and local authorities in economic development measures.

E.   Policy Conclusions

In Japan the process of urban concentration at the national and metropolitan levels has been carried to a high degree when compared with other OECD countries. The first point is illustrated by the close proximity of the three major urban centres, the second by the high densities of Japanese cities. The two aspects of urban concentration have common roots in the rural to urban migration, reinforced by industrial growth policies, mainly in the 1950s and 1960s.

To achieve balanced development, broad policies on national development and land use planning are in place through successive updating of national plans and associated legislation. There is a consistent theme in these national policies in favour of the dispersal of industrial activity, based on the concept of growth poles, coupled with restrictions on development in the major metropolitan areas. In practice economic and market forces, combined with the lack of strong instruments for implementation of national plans, have tended to intensify urban concentration in the metropolitan areas on the southern seaboard of central Honshu.

As a partial and more achievable alternative, some policy emphasis is now being given to dispersal within the metropolitan areas. The aim is to promote multi-centred cities, with different functional characteristics, which might reduce some of the pressure on the older city centres. The success of this approach will depend on firm guidance and encouragement by national and local governments. In Tokyo, reducing the pressure for office development within the Yamanote line, by establishing sub-centres backed by incentives to develop there, is an urgent priority.

When the population figures are compared with the objectives of policy it can be seen that only now does a move towards a more balanced population structure seem to be emerging. In the period 1975-80 the population of all prefectures, except Tokyo with a 0.5 per cent decline, increased for the first time in the last 10 years. There are signs that industrial and urban policy are now working together to achieve balance, as opposed to earlier decades when despite the former policies concentration occurred.

The value of urban policies which pursue a consistent line in the long term has been shown. Industrial policy has changed to supporting growth sectors and "high tech" industries, which are seeking locations away from existing metropolitan areas. Existing deconcentration policies will need to be maintained accompanied by a switch of emphasis from the secondary to the tertiary sector. If this is not successful the probability is that the three metropolitan areas will become even more strongly differentiated from the rest of Japan. Already Tokyo has 27 per cent of all the tertiary employment in Japan.

The technopolises, building on a longstanding tradition of new towns, even if all fully implemented by 1990, would only cater for approximately 1-2 per cent of the Japanese population. However, signs exist that the central government may be willing to set an example by moving some of its functions from central Tokyo. Tsukuba new town shows what can be achieved in this respect. Other OECD countries have experience of policies offering financial incentives to companies which transfer offices from capital cities. These can particularly be successfully applied to non-headquarters type office functions.

The second major switch of emphasis, which again is already taking place but needs to be accelerated, is the restructuring of the metropolitan areas, now that growth will mainly come from within by natural increase. The accent, therefore, needs to be moved from national urban policies which were not successful in stopping unbalanced growth of Tokaido in the first place, to seeking balance within the Tokyo metropolitan area. Since 1975 Tokyo has strengthened its position in relation to Osaka and Nagoya and it is particularly in the national capital region that special measures need to be applied. A less centralised metropolitan structure, based on sub-centres either in or near Tokyo itself and the growth of medium-sized towns in the wider metropolitan area, will need to be supported by investment in the transportation infrastructure and social capital in the growing towns, to make them attractive alternatives to Tokyo.

NOTES AND REFERENCES

1. Economic Analysis of Urbanisation in Japan, N. Sakashita in *Urban Growth Policies in the 1980s*, OECD, Paris, 1983.

2. *Academic Preference for Decentralisation in Japan*, H. Nakamura, ISA, 1983.

3. Japan: Towards a New Metropolitan policy, S. Yamaguchi, *Cities*, August 1984.

4. *The Three Largest Cities in Japan*, M. Sawamoto, Kobayashi International Urban Policy Research Foundation, June 1985.

5. The Japanese National Settlement System, T. Yamaguchi in *Urbanisation and Settlement Systems: International Perspective*, Bourne, Sinclair and Dziewarski (Eds), Oxford University Press, 1984.

6. *Metamorphosis of the Capital and Evolution of the Urban System in Japan*, M. Miyakawa, Ekistics, March/April 1983.

7. Japan follows the New Town Path, L. A. Allen, *Town and Country Planning*, November 1983.

Chapter 4

THE RATIONAL USE OF LAND

Developing the conclusions of the previous chapter, that existing programmes to encourage growth outside and discourage growth inside the metropolitan areas should be maintained and even enhanced, they are unlikely on the evidence of past experience and predicted trends to achieve a rapid large-scale national redistribution of the urban population. The accent of future urban policies in Japan, therefore, switches towards the restructuring of the large metropolitan areas, particularly the Kanto plain, which has Tokyo as its focus. The demographic statistics indicate that the process of metropolitan deconcentration in Japan has been in train for some time and it is forecast to continue (Table 13). The future use of land in the metropolitan regions, therefore, becomes a pivotal urban policy issue[1]. It will be necessary to harness the deconcentration trends, present for both housing and employment, to the other public policy goals, higher levels of urban infrastructure and environment improvement, which are considered later in this report. In turn lower densities in the existing core cities should facilitate urban improvement processes there, alongside the improved standards sought in the newly developed area.

Table 13. **Metropolitan residential land forecasts, 1986-1990**

	National capital	Kinki	Chubu	Japan
Demand (ha)	14 500	7 600	7 000	60 700
Houses on new sites (million)	1.06	0.54	0.38	3.60
Land area per house (m²)	164	149	188	189
Net Area (m²)	55	55	55	56
Apartments (%)	46	35	25	36
Supply (ha)	13 200	7 100	6 600	57 900
Public supply	3 800	2 300	800	11 000
Land readjustment	4 000	1 600	3 100	20 000
Private supply	4 900	3 200	2 700	26 900
Expected shortfall (ha)	1 300	500	400	2 800

Source: Ministry of Construction.

A. Land Resources

Of direct relevance in this context is one of the main objectives of urban policy in Japan, as identified in Chapter 2, concerning the rational use of land. This is an especially important

Table 14. **Land use in Japan, 1965-1985**

10 000 km^2

	1965	1975	1985
Urban	85	122	148
Roads	82	97	112
Agricultural	643	575	611
Moorland	64	41	26
Forests	2 516	2 518	2 482

Source: Ministry of Construction.

Table 15. **OECD countries: population densities, 1983**

Inhabitants per km^2

Netherlands	385	Spain	76
Belgium	323	Greece	75
Japan	320	Turkey	61
Germany	247	Ireland	50
United Kingdom	230	United States	25
Italy	189	Sweden	19
Switzerland	158	Finland	14
Luxembourg	141	Norway	13
Denmark	119	New Zealand	12
Portugal	109	Australia	2
France	100	Canada	2
Austria	90	Iceland	2

Source: OECD, FAO.

Table 16. **OECD countries[1]: GDP per unit area, 1983**

1 000 U.S.$ per km^2

Netherlands	3 889	Spain	317
Japan	3 116	Greece	264
Germany	2 673	Ireland	261
Belgium	2 624	Portugal	226
Switzerland	2 442	Sweden	223
United Kingdom	1 884	Norway	179
Denmark	1 330	Finland	162
Luxembourg	1 232	New Zealand	86
Italy	1 220	Turkey	65
France	952	Canada	35
Austria	811	Iceland	23
United States	359	Australia	20

1. Gross domestic product, at current prices and exchange rates, per square kilometre of land.
Source: OECD, FAO.

consideration, because the land surface of Japan is being urbanised at a rapid rate (Table 14). Also, land in Japan is particularly densely occupied and utilised. Comparative figures for other OECD countries illustrate the high ranking of Japan in terms of the density of both population and economic activity (Tables 15 and 16). There have been some large scale land reclamation schemes, such as Port Island at Kobe, which have made an important qualitative contribution to urban land supply in the past. However, these are unlikely greatly to affect the overall land supply situation, in comparison to the predicted growth of population and economic activity.

Account also has to be taken in these figures of the physical geography of Japan. It is estimated that only one-fifth of the Japanese land area is habitable as compared, for example, to two-thirds in France and Germany and half in the United States. Certainly, because of the concentration of urban development in Tokaido, general urban densities in Japan far exceed those of other OECD countries. In 1980, for example, 60 million Japanese, over half of the national population, were living in 10 000 km^2 comprising the Densely Inhabited Districts (DIDs). This is an area slightly less than the Ile de France, the Paris Region, which is the most densely populated in France, with 10 million inhabitants.

Besides the view that land is a resource, particularly evident in a country such as Japan which is not well endowed with natural resources, other considerations come into play in setting out the rational use of land as an objective of urban policy. The first is to increase the efficiency of urban infrastructure provision and the second is the question of the desirable degree of national self-sufficiency in food. In this context the waste that occurs as land awaiting development is either under-used, misused or unused for long periods is of particular significance. Factors which play a significant part in other countries when seeking rational land policies, such as the compatibility of different land uses, the social differences between urban and rural communities and aesthetic considerations, relating to the lack of a clear urban/rural boundary, do not appear to carry the same weight in Japan as in other OECD countries.

It is not just the dense overall occupation and the intense productivity of the inhabitable area that define the challenge to the Japanese of making the optimum use of their limited land resources. Fragmentation of land occurs both in terms of geography and ownership. Japan officially consists of 3922 islands. Transport links are being improved between the main island of Honshu and Hokkaido, with the construction of a rail tunnel, road and rail bridges between Honshu and Shikoku and more generally through the extension of air transport. The inevitably restricted nature of intercommunication, particularly between the four main islands, is not only an impediment to the balanced development discussed in the previous chapter, but to achieving a national perspective on the rational use of the land surface of Japan.

The other aspect of land fragmentation, which presents a severe challenge to securing an orderly process of land conversion, is that of the small size of the average land holding. During the period 1945-50 the ownership of large agricultural estates was divided among tenant farmers. This has resulted in the average size of agricultural holding being less than one hectare. In one sense this was a return to a traditional pattern. Most of the large estates had only come into being in the latter half of the last century. Taxes became payable in cash rather than kind and cottage industries declined in the face of competition from industrially produced goods. As a result farming bankrupties rose severely and holdings were amalgamated.

Linked to the earlier point about the limited overall national supply of land, the fragmented pattern of land ownership in both existing and prospective urban areas poses particular difficulties to achieving rational patterns of urban land use. The fragmented land ownership in Japan is reflected in a very high proportion of residential development schemes being of less than one hectare, with each house on a very small site, the so-called "minikaihatsu". The additional reasons for this style of development include the exemption from control and price regulations; little new infrastructure need be provided; and the owner wishing to retain the remaining part of the usually part-time agricultural holding. These points are discussed later in this chapter.

The outcome of the points discussed above – the intensity of use and the difficulties of land assembly – is that land prices in Japan are high and have become an important focus of political attention[2]. Statistics for land price by region and use not only show how high land prices are, but also how they vary with the size of urban settlement concerned (Table 17). The statistics also show that high land prices are concentrated in the three large metropolitan areas, particularly in Tokyo. Figures for 1985 show that land prices are beginning to rise faster in the National Capital Region than previously. Also, the rate of increase there is faster than elsewhere in Japan, notably for office development but also for housing.

Table 17. **Urban land prices, 1985**

Yen per m^2

	Residential	Proposed residential	Residential land in UCAs	Commercial	Industrial
Tokyo	196 500	48 700	36 200	1 299 400	92 500
Osaka	168 900	47 300	45 400	822 200	124 900
Nagoya	97 100	30 100	38 300	332 700	58 500
Cities 500 000+	74 200	26 900	23 400	394 800	51 900
Cities 300 000+	71 600	29 800	25 900	344 300	40 000
Others	54 000	24 200	19 900	213 000	30 700

Source: Ministry of Construction.

In Japan land costs contribute approximately 35 per cent to house prices. In other OECD countries land prices typically contribute between 15 and 20 per cent. In the early seventies residential land prices in Japan increased sharply, relative to other price movements, in response to excess liquidity and the expectation of high capital gains. In recent years land prices have shown greater stability and are beginning to fall in real terms (Diagram 4). But increases have still exceeded those in the consumer and wholesale price indices (Diagram 5). In comparison with earnings, however, land prices have risen at a slower rate. The reasons for the recent pattern of stability lie in the measures which were introduced following the steep 1972-74 price rise and the subsequent fall-off in housing starts.

Based on the rise in land prices for a considerable number of years, land is seen as an investment with which neither money nor any other type of capital asset can compete. This orientation of wealth formation towards the ownership of land has drawbacks for the revitalisation of inner city areas, as well as on the overall effective use of land. It limits the introduction of both gradual and comprehensive schemes for redevelopment.

Policy measures to confront high land prices, as reflected in the high price of housing, have concentrated on low interest rate, long-term loans. These have enabled prospective home owners to continue to afford housing, in the face of steadily rising prices. However, by themselves, measures to stimulate the demand for housing have not been sufficient to alleviate

Diagram 4

LAND PRICE CHANGES, 1956-1984

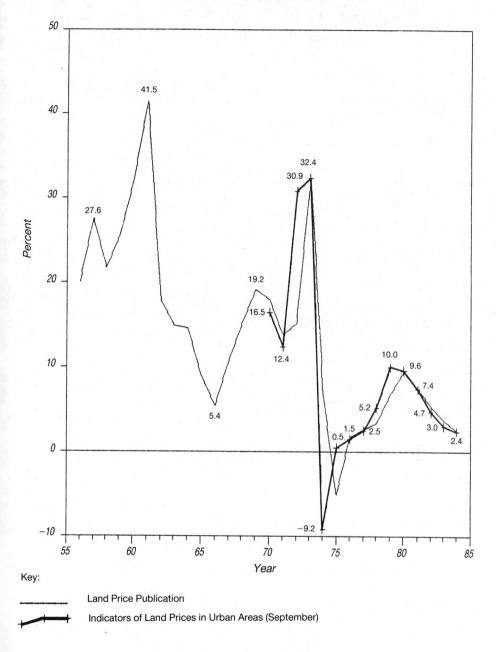

Key:

_____ Land Price Publication

┼━━━┼ Indicators of Land Prices in Urban Areas (September)

Sources: *National Land Agency, Japan Real Estate Research Institute*

Diagram 5

LAND PRICE INDEX, 1955-1984

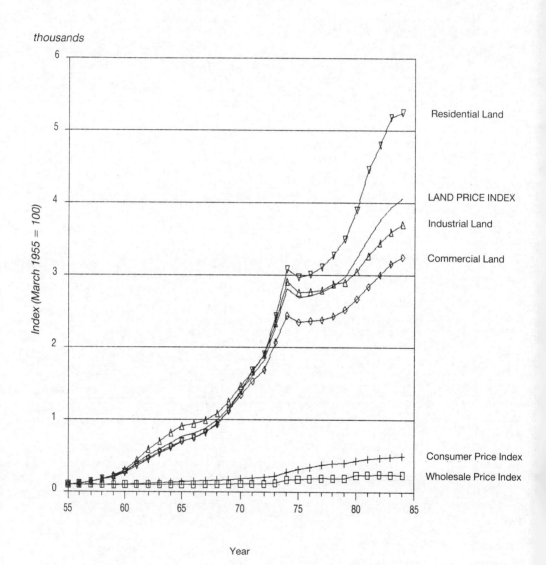

52

the housing situation. Complementary policies to improve the supply of land, by encouraging owners to bring forward sites for development, have not been so actively pursued. Despite legislation, such as the Special Measures for Facilitating the Supply of Residential Land in Major Metropolitan Areas Act, 1975, the high degree of uncertainty about land availability has encouraged speculation and raised land prices over large parts of growing metropolitan areas[3]. A further, special feature of the Japanese housing situation is that, until recently, the second hand house market was not well developed and did not act as a constraint on the market for new housing.

B. Urban Planning Legislation

Japan has a long tradition of urban planning legislation[4] including the Tokyo City Remodelling Ordinance, 1888, and the City Planning and Urban Building Acts of 1919. Although applied initially to the six largest cities, by 1933 the legislation had been amended so that it could apply everywhere in Japan. However, the powers to do so rested with central government. It was not until towards the end of the main period of recent urbanisation that eight principal categories of land use were introduced, in the City Planning Act, 1968. Other features of the 1968 Act were the devolution of plan making powers to the prefectural and municipal levels; the introduction of public participation procedures; and the establishment of a heirarchy, whereby city plans have to conform to metropolitan plans, where they exist, and also to national and prefectural plans.

The recognised territorial unit for urban planning is the "city planning area". This may cover a large area including several municipalities and the boundaries need not necessarily coincide with existing administrative units. The Prefectural Governor sets the limits of city planning areas, after consultation with the municipal representatives and with the approval of the Minister of Construction. The Governor is also obliged to review conditions and trends in city planning areas every five years. City planning areas have been designated principally in the case of built-up areas with a population of more than 10 000; areas with mainly industrial employment; and tracts of land set aside for the extension of metropolitan areas. After the designation of a city planning area, plans are drawn up by the local administrations, although the major final decisions on the plans remain with the Prefectural Governor.

The central feature of the 1968 Act consists of the sub-division of city planning areas into Urbanisation Promotion Areas (UPAs) and Urbanisation Control Areas (UCAs), to quote Article 7: "in order to prevent disorderly development and realise development according to a plan". The UPAs comprise the existing urban areas (defined as having a population of 5 000+ and a density of 40 pph+) plus the areas planned to be built up within approximately ten years. Areas liable to disasters, excellent farmland and areas of outstanding natural scenery are excluded from UPAs. The UCAs consist of the areas where urbanisation should be limited.

At the end of March 1984, while the Act applied to 349 city planning areas covering 874 municipalities and three-quarters of the total population (89M), only in 324 of these areas had the division into UPAs and UCAs been decided. The UPAs covered a quarter and the UCAs the remaining three-quarters of the total land area involved. The Prefectural Governor delimits the UPAs and UCAs following government approval, which often entails detailed negotiations with the Ministry of Agriculture. In principle, decisions are reviewed every five years, but in 1980 the City Planning Act, 1968, was amended to introduce district planning to provide a more detailed approach to securing urban development and redevelopment.

Compliance with city plans is ensured by the development permission that an intending developer in a UPA or UCA must obtain from the Prefectural Governor. However, in accordance with Article 29 of the 1968 Act, development permission is not required in the following cases:

i) In UPAs, development operations involving less than 1 000 m², (Prefectural regulations can lower this limit to 300 m²);
ii) In city planning areas not divided into UPAs and UCAs, development operations involving less than 3 000 m²;
iii) In UCAs, construction intended for farming, forestry or fishing activities, or for housing associated with these activities; and
iv) Development decided upon by the central government, prefectures, designated cities and various public agencies concerning the provision of public facilities.

When development permission is necessary, acceptance depends on the Prefectural Governor, who must consider the following two aims: formation of an undesirable urban environment must be prevented and a certain standard must be guaranteed; and erratic urban sprawl must be avoided.

In exceptional cases, the Prefectural Governor may grant permission for development in UCAs, provided that it meets the two aims. Land provided with road access and sewerage is usually judged to comply. Permission is generally given where the developer is prepared to provide the appropriate infrastructure and where a large scale development (20 hectares+) is proposed. However, prefectural regulations can lower this limit to 5 hectares. The Agricultural Promotion Area Improvement Act, 1969, was enacted in order to identify the areas in which agriculture is promoted. In the agricultural promotion areas local governments designate "farm land areas" in which the conversion of agricultural land to other uses is restricted. However, exemptions are permitted under conditions which are stipulated in the Act. There is a high rate of conversion of land from agricultural to residential use in Japan, with over half of the change being recorded in the three major metropolitan areas (Tables 18 and 19). Within the UPAs, the city plan must define land use zones covered by regulations, of which the most important are a volume ratio; a coverage ratio; and maximum building height.

Table 18. **Agricultural land converted to residential use in urbanisation promotion areas, 1972-1982**

Hectares

	Japan		3 Metropolitan areas	
	Area	Annual rate of change %	Area	Annual rate of change %
1972	10 299	24.2	5 387	10.1
1973	10 275	−0.2	4 723	−12.3
1974	6 016	−41.5	2 878	−39.1
1975	5 281	−12.2	2 695	−6.4
1976	5 347	1.2	2 685	−0.4
1977	5 054	−5.5	2 534	−5.6
1978	4 959	−1.9	2 481	−2.1
1979	5 247	5.8	2 619	5.6
1980	4 360	−16.9	2 221	−15.2
1981	3 856	−11.6	1 980	−10.9
1982	3 943	2.3	2 140	8.1

Source: Ministry of Construction.

Table 19. **Conversion of agricultural land to development, selected OECD countries, 1960-1980**

Percentage of Agricultural Land

	1960-1970	1970-1980
Japan	7.3	5.7
Denmark	3.0	1.5
France	1.8	1.1
Germany	2.5	2.4
Netherlands	4.3	3.6
New Zealand	0.5	–
Sweden	1.0	1.0
United Kingdom	1.8	0.6
United States	0.8	2.8

Source: OECD Environmental Data Compendium, 1985.

Zoning decisions are generally taken at municipal level, with decisions concerning the major cities to be made by the Prefectural Governor.

Overlaying the system of urban plans introduced by the City Planning Act, 1968, is a series of prefectural land use plans, which indicate five types of land use – City Areas, Agricultural Areas, Forestry Areas, Natural Park Areas and Nature Conservation Areas at a 1:50 000 scale. Based on the National Land Use Plan, administered by the National Land Agency, the production of national and prefectural land use plans, together with the City Planning Act requirements for plans, produces a complex situation, with the inevitable difficulties of comprehension and co-ordination between different plans.

Besides its plan-producing responsibilities, the NLA also administers a system of land price registration and publication which, because of its novelty, has attracted considerable interest in other OECD countries. The Land Price Publication Act, 1969, requires the annual publication of land prices together with details of the land concerned. The objective is to provide factual information to help stabilise the land market. The system was introduced in stages beginning with the three large metropolitan regions, but in 1974 UCAs were included. In 1983 some 17 000 prices were listed nationally in Japan. Prefecture Governors have powers to designate regulation areas for periods of up to five years. In these areas land transactions need to be registered with the Governor and the contract will not be effective without such registration. The areas to be designated would be those where there are a large number of speculative land transactions or where prices were rapidly rising. So far no regulation areas have been designated because land prices have shown greater stability in recent years.

In all areas land transactions have to be reported which are above a certain area, for example, more than 2 000 m^2 in UPAs. The price and proposed usage have to be reported. If the price violates the advisory standard set by the Prefecture, then this information is given to those conducting the transaction and can be published, with the objective that the publicity will act as a sanction. In 1984 there were 39 455 registrations, no advice was given in respect of 36 002 registrations, 1 223 registrations were approved after the price was reduced following Prefectorial advice and 2 227 were withdrawn. Only in three cases was the advisory standard not observed.

Land use regulations of the type described in the previous section tend to be of limited effectiveness in OECD countries unless backed up by a complementary system of taxation.

55

The City Planning Act, 1968, and the National Land Use Planning Act, 1974, have therefore been supplemented by a number of measures, introduced in the early 1970s, to tax land hoarding and short-term capital gains made by companies from land sales:

- i) Where land is disposed of less than ten years after acquisition a 40 per cent capital gains tax is imposed;
- ii) Where land is held by corporations for less than ten years there is a 20 per cent capital gains tax, in addition to standard corporation tax, unless the land is sold for public purposes or for the supply of housing lots of an acceptable standard; and
- iii) Where the total area of land acquired within one year exceeds a certain area, a special land possession tax of 3 per cent of the value of the land acquired is imposed.

In addition, there are exemptions to capital gains tax, which are designed to encourage the bringing forward of land for development. If land is expropriated Y 30 million is not taxable. If the land is to be used for public facilities Y 30 million is excluded and for housing in city planning areas Y 15 million. In 1983 further tax concessions were introduced in which tax postponement was permitted on profits from land sold to become part of a large scale development and also to encourage medium and high rise construction. Further, in land readjustment projects, discussed below, the first Y 15 million of profits is exempted from taxation in certain circumstances.

Taxes and subsidies also aim to encourage owner occupation by reducing the market cost of acquisition and by the provision of long-term loans. Interest rates for housing purchase have recently been about 3 per cent below market rates. This may have aggravated the land price situation, by increasing demand at a time when measures to assist the supply side have not been actively pursued. In 1973, specified municipalities in the three metropolitan areas were given the power to tax agricultural land in UPAs at residential values. However, where land is intended to be farmed for a period of more than ten years exemptions are granted and these are widespread. Because of their low productivity, these agricultural holdings tend to have a low valuation.

C. Land Assembly

The assembly of sites for development is an essential part of the process of achieving a rational use of land. Japan has a range of mechanisms available including land readjustment, "Kukaku-seiri" (Diagram 6), which has attracted interest in other OECD countries[5].

With an average size of 35 hectares, land readjustment projects initiated in Japan in the last decade applied to an annual average of 5 700 hectares. Half of these projects arose from private initiatives (individuals or land readjustment associations) and half were promoted by the public sector (municipalities, prefectures, public corporations). The latter projects are generally considerably larger, 150 hectares as against 20 hectares for private projects, and more complex. For these reasons they take almost twice as long to complete – nine years, as against five years for private projects. The smaller schemes in existing urban areas have more the purpose of rationalising layouts and providing new facilities, than assembling land.

The land readjustment technique originated in the Arable Land Consolidation Act of 1899, based on German legislation. It was given impetus by the large-scale urban rebuilding necessary after the Kanto earthquake of 1923 and extended by the Land Readjustment Act, 1954. Government subsidies are given to assist the preparation and implementation of the projects, including moving existing buildings to new sites. However, many owners choose to put the subsidy towards the cost of a new house. The subsidies come from the road

Diagram 6

LAND REAJUSTMENT SYSTEM

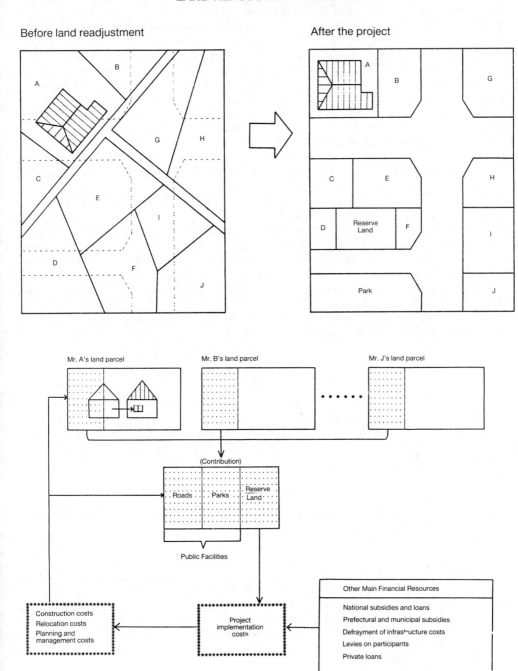

Before land readjustment

After the project

Mr. A's land parcel

Mr. B's land parcel

Mr. J's land parcel

(Contribution)

Roads   Parks   Reserve Land

: Public Facilities

Construction costs
Relocation costs
Planning and management costs

Project implementation costs

Other Main Financial Resources

National subsidies and loans
Prefectural and municipal subsidies
Defrayment of infrastructure costs
Levies on participants
Private loans

improvement budget of the MOC, but although the improvement of the road layout is one objective this is a very limited perspective on land readjustment. Considerable public savings are made in the supply of infrastructure and services, evidence of the potential effectiveness in Japan of public/private co-operation in urban development. To illustrate the possible scale of activities, a major scheme in Yokohama, undertaken by the Japan Housing and Urban Development Corporation, involved 1 300 hectares and 7 200 land owners.

However, there seems to be a strong tendency to locate projects further and further out on the fringes of metropolitan areas, thereby encouraging the spread of urban development. Land readjustment there is easier than in existing urban areas. The land requires neither extensive preparatory work nor the moving or demolition of existing buildings, and projects can be implemented more quickly. Further, while on the urban fringe subsidies are less, the sale of surplus land can cover the cost of the project, despite the requirement to grant land free of charge for public facilities. In existing urban areas the requirement to provide land for roads and other public facilities can have the adverse effect of producing very narrow, small sites. To avoid this situation new measures to assist the amalgamation of separate land holdings are required.

Approximately one-third of newly urbanised land in UPAs is covered by land readjustment projects. The number of and area covered by publicly initiated projects have fallen in the last twenty years, while private projects have grown in number and maintained their area (Table 20). Significantly, the public projects are mainly located in areas which are already built-up or partly so. This means that they are more complicated, needing more time and work, and requiring heavier rates of subsidy for higher levels of expenditure. Also, land readjustment projects are not a guarantee of immediate development and the sites provided often remain undeveloped. Of the land readjustment projects carried out and provided with the necessary infrastructure, plots amounting to 18 400 hectares remain idle: enough for a full year of residential building at existing rates.

Table 20. **Land readjustment projects, 1965-1984**

Body responsible	Number of projects			Land area (hectares)		
	1965	1975	1984	1965	1975	1984
Individuals and Groups of Individuals	9	33	20	345	776	121
Associations	38	109	148	2 190	1 714	2 265
Municipalities and Prefectures	58	40	37	4 241	2 287	1 500
Housing and Urban Development Corporation	1	1	5	702	68	301
Regional Housing Supply Corporations	0	0	1	0	0	332
Total	106	183	211	7 478	4 845	4 519

For specifically urban projects in existing cities, the Urban Renewal Act, 1969, discussed in the next chapter, instituted Category I urban redevelopment projects, founded on the principles of owner participation; a more intensive use of land; and the title conversion system (Diagram 7). These projects may be privately or publicly initiated. The system entitles each owner or title holder to co-ownership of the reallocated land and, after demolition and higher density rebuilding, to a pro rata share of the floor space in the new building. The system makes it easier to build co-operative blocks of flats and condominiums and promotes community

Diagram 7

TITLE CONVERSION SYSTEM

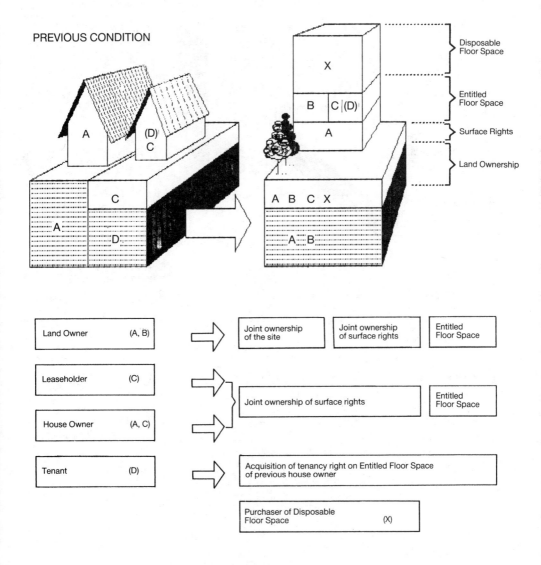

Diagram 8

EQUIVALENT EXCHANGE SYSTEM

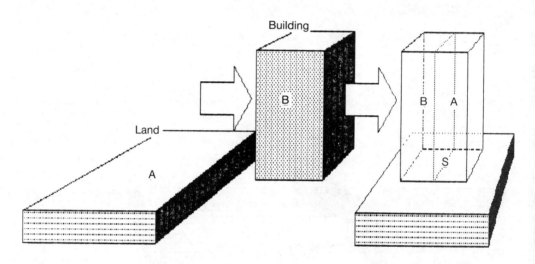

Share after completion of
the building

Developer's   Land owner's
share   share

Building

B

Land

A

B   A

S

Co-ownership in pro-
portion to each share

Land owner's share = $S \times \dfrac{A}{A/B}$

Developer's share = $S \times \dfrac{B}{A/B}$

A :   Total price of land

B :   Total construction cost

S :   Total floor space of multi-storey apartment

stability by allowing residents to remain in the same area. Based on tax legislation, the equivalent exchange system, which is closely related to the title conversion system, is designed to achieve the same ends. In this case the agreement is between a land owner and a private developer (Diagram 8).

Compulsory public land acquisition is another way of overcoming difficulties presented when key areas of land are not available for development. As in other OECD countries, powers of eminent domain have existed in Japan for some time and were reinforced in the City Planning Act, 1968. However, the Narita Airport project, for example, encountered difficulties in the course of compulsory land acquisition procedures. Consensus seeking is, therefore, the favoured approach to securing the release of land in circumstances where owners are initially unwilling to sell land. In Urban Renewal Schemes two-thirds of the owners need to be in agreement, although consideration is being given to reducing this to 51 per cent.

D. Policy Conclusions

Japan is facing a period of urban deconcentration. To deal effectively with this process, involving both the construction of new development and the redevelopment of older areas, it needs to be handled in an orderly way. This can also help to ensure the efficient provision of urban infrastructure and to safeguard land resources, as well as to meet aspirations for an improved standard of urban living and environment, discussed in later chapters. National public policy methods of seeking to secure the rational use of urban land can be divided into three categories, all of which are well represented in Japan. First, town planning legislation dealing with the development process, secondly, fiscal measures affecting the holding and sale of land and, thirdly, measures assisting the process of land assembly.

The Japanese Government has shown considerable ingenuity and persistence in pursuing the objective of the rational use of land. Radical departures from the current approach are not advocated although, as was pointed out earlier, changes to the agricultural support system and to the balance between rural and urban interests are needed, if the process of metropolitan development is to be handled effectively. With another 18 million urban residents to be housed by the year 2000 – almost two more cities the size of Tokyo – the urban policy challenges in Japan will not diminish. The main priority is to increase the supply of land in areas scheduled for development. As part of the 1985 economic measures to stimulate domestic demand, public sector sites suitable for development are to be released. The Government can continue to set an example in this respect.

To complement these measures, it is also important for policies to promote appropriate urban uses on vacant and agricultural land within Urbanisation Promotion Areas. In other areas urban containment policies are important for a number of reasons. They assist the efficient use of land and, by limiting random urban development, allow high quality agricultural land to be retained and good agricultural practices to be promoted. Urban policies and new measures such as Agricultural Promotion Areas have begun to assist urban containment. At the same time containment helps to prevent urban decline by limiting the choices for new development, ensuring that the regeneration of an existing urban area remains a competitive option.

However, within Urbanisation Control Areas there is a wide range of exemptions that are not controlled. The distinction between "promotion" and "control", even if it was more rigorously applied, is not sophisticated enough to achieve effective urban containment. A further refinement of the designations is needed to ensure that there are areas where there is an effective policy of no development. Institutional changes are less easy to evaluate. But it also seems that the procedures for land readjustment projects and for obtaining permission for development could be streamlined to increase land supply.

To achieve an improvement in the land supply situation, particularly underused land in the large metropolitan areas, action should be taken to identify such land and incentives introduced to bring it into effective urban use. To support these tax measures, central government should become more actively involved in securing and releasing land to the private sector and, more generally, monitoring the supply of land for urban development.

Changes of policy are also required to land and property taxation to support these urban planning measures. The tax on the holding of land that has been allocated for development needs to be progressively increased. This applies particularly in the three metropolitan areas. The increase in the rate of taxation on land holding needs to be complemented by the reduction of taxes which discourage the sale of land. These changes in taxation would initiate the land assembly process and make its subsequent progress easier.

A general property tax, reflecting the value of land, is a better way to secure the release of land and to stabilise land prices than a capital gains tax at the time the land is sold. However, owners might be encouraged to sell land in small parcels over a period of time to meet their tax obligations. Therefore, a minimum residential plot size needs to be introduced, which would also have the effect of improving housing standards, while not unduly influencing land prices and the amount of land required for urban development. A further change of approach is necessary to avoid the situation in which the smaller a development operation, the easier it is to avoid planning control. Also, charges need not rise proportionately with the complexity, duration and scale of the project as, for example, the proportion of land to be ceded free for public uses which currently increases with the area of site involved.

NOTES AND REFERENCES

1. Housing and Land Policies in Japan, S. Ishihara in *Urban Growth Policies in the 1980s*, OECD, Paris, 1983.

2. Urbanization and Land Prices: The Case of Tokyo, Y. Kanayama in *Economic Growth and Resources: Problems related to Japan*, Ed. S. Tsuru, Macmillan Press, London, 1980.

3. *Urban Sprawl and Planning Failure – Some Reflections on the Japanese Case*, M. Hebbert, University of Sheffield, 1985.

4. Metropolitan Planning in Japan, J. Alden, *Town Planning Review*, Vol. 55, No. 1, 1984.

5. Learning from the Japanese, I. Masser, *Town and Country Planning*, London, January 1984.

Chapter 5

HOUSING AND URBAN REVITALISATION

From considering policies dealing with the location of urbanisation – balanced development and the rational use of land – this chapter turns its attention to the quality of urban areas. Residential neighbourhoods constitute the major part of cities and are where the majority of people spend most of their time. Housing policies, therefore, directly influence residents' day-by-day perceptions of urban life. As such the standard of the residential environment is an important part of the general welfare of a nation.

A. Legislation and Institutions

The general aim of housing policy in Japan "is to provide housing that will enable the people to live securely in a good residential environment taking into account the family composition, the process of household growth and the neighbourhood". Specific objectives are set out in the 5-year construction programmes, prepared by the MOC, concerning minimum housing standards, average housing standards and standards for the residential environment. This latter requirement was only introduced in the 4th programme (1981-5) and illustrates the growing awareness of the links between housing policies and urban environmental quality.

The Housing Loan Corporation Act, 1950, and the Publicly Operated Housing Act, 1951, form the basis for housing policy in Japan. Housing legislation has been developed gradually since 1951, moving from laws and regulations designed to redevelop war damaged cities, when one-quarter of the population was homeless, to a system established to respond to housing shortages and large scale migration to cities. By 1970 the number of houses exceeded the number of households and the emphasis was switched to improving standards. Japanese housing policy is also becoming more integrated and co-ordinated with urban planning and land policies. The merger, in 1981, of the New Town Development Corporation (set up in 1975) and the Japan Housing Corporation (set up in 1955), to form the Japan Housing and Urban Development Corporation (JHUDC), signalled this new orientation.

The Housing Construction Programme Act, 1966, forms the main legislative framework for housing policy implementation in Japan. In the most recent five year programmes (1971/75, 1976/80, 1981/85), the targets for the number of housing units to be constructed were, respectively, 9.6, 8.6 and 7.7 million. In the first two of these programmes 40 per cent of the housing units were to be publicly financed and in the recently completed programme 45 per cent. Between 1971 and 1980 production was 85-90 per cent of the programme targets and, although the 1981/5 target was again lowered in comparison to the previous programme period, the target is not likely to be achieved. Nevertheless, in Japan 6 per cent of GDP is spent

Table 21. **Housing construction 1946-1985**

Thousands

	Private sector[1]	Public sector	Total
1946-50	2 071	466	2 537
1951-55	1 189	359	1 548
1956-60	2 052	531	2 583
1961-65	3 167	819	3 986
1966-70	5 261	1 478	6 739
1971-75	6 836	1 444	8 280
1976-80	6 596	1 102	7 698
1981-85	5 274	846	6 120
Total	32 446	7 045	39 491

1. Private Sector includes HLC financed housing.
2. 1985 figures are estimates.
Source: Ministry of Construction.

on housing, a higher proportion than in other OECD countries. In the last 40 years the ratio of private sector to public sector provision has been 4.5:1, but in the 1980s the public sector contribution has declined (Table 21).

The main institutions in the housing field are the Housing Loan Corporation (HLC), which provides finance for buying owner-occupied housing; and the JHUDC, which mainly provides public rented housing and housing for sale for middle income households in metropolitan areas. Local government bodies also provide "Publicly Operated Housing", in the form of rental units for low-income families. MOC financially supports both Corporations and gives subsidies to local Housing Supply Corporations to construct Publicly Operated Housing. Local government bodies, which operate at the level of the prefectures and the nine "designated" cities, also build housing for sale or rent. Employers also provide housing for their staff and it is estimated that 5 per cent of the housing stock consists of this form of tenure. The JHUDC's direct contribution of 20-25 000 housing units per annum is a modest one, though concentrated in the three major metropolitan and the Kita-Kyushu areas.

B. Housing Finance

Financial support for private housing arises from both the public and private sectors. HLC loans are the main form of government assistance. Although the proportion of loans by private financial institutions has been falling, it still exceeds half the total. Private finance for housing in Japan is based on funds allocated by the credit and capital market, through a variety of channels and organisations. The conditions of private loans vary with the type of private institution, but in general they are on less favourable terms than loans from the HLC. The private sector has recently responded to the needs of house buyers by adopting floating rate and variable term mortgages.

The budget of the MOC for housing purposes has been constrained in recent years at approximately Y 900 billion, the proportion of the annual, national budget being approximately 1.8 per cent in recent years. The total amount of loans issued by the HLC in 1984 was Y 3.4 trillion, while the MOC contribution, to reduce interest rates charged by the

Corporation, amounted to Y 286 billion. In the case of the JHUDC the government contribution amounted to approximately half of that Corporation's 1984 budget of Y 1.5 trillion. However, the MOC's contribution was limited to Y 150 billion, again with the objective of lowering interest rates. The remainder of JHUDC's funds are raised either on the private market or from bond issues.

In OECD countries, housing subsidies play a major part in the implementation of housing policy objectives. In Japan public housing is subsidised, while subsidies in the form of fixed-term (25-30 years), low-interest loans from HLC to owner occupiers also play a considerable role. These loans, offered on a nominal annuity basis, imply that housing outlays are heavier in relation to disposable income of households in the period immediately after purchase. This initial level of housing expenditure is often prohibitive. However, over time increases in household income tend to result in a sharp decrease in the ratio between housing expenditure and disposable income.

Many OECD countries have housing finance systems whereby the subsidy element either decreases over time or is subject to changing economic conditions. Japan has recently seen the introduction of similar schemes. Interest rates are reduced during the first ten years of a mortgage and payments can be deferred during the first five years. The former scheme was introduced in 1982, while the latter dates from 1979. This is particularly important under conditions of financial restraint on public budgets. In this way subsidy systems can be transformed from static policy instruments to become incorporated in the overall economic performance of households and countries. Urban housing conditions have to be viewed in a long-term perspective. The annual production of housing is small compared to the existing housing stock and it takes a long time before housing supply corresponds to higher levels of income. Further, because a high priority has been given to industrial development in Japan, housing production has not increased in line with growth in the economy.

C. Housing Standards

While, from a statistical viewpoint, Japan has an excess supply of housing units when compared with households, the situation is not so satisfactory as it would appear. One of the striking characteristics of Japanese housing is the large number of vacant houses, particularly considering that 40 years ago the housing shortage was estimated at 4.2M units. The vacancy ratio has increased from 4 per cent of the total housing stock in 1968 to 8.6 per cent in 1983 (Table 22). The majority of the vacant housing is of small, substandard, traditional wooden construction in the major metropolitan areas. So both nationally and in the three largest cities

Table 22. **Housing units and households in Japan, 1968-1983**

Thousands

	1968	1973	1978	1983
Households	25 320	29 651	32 835	35 197
Dwelling units	25 591	31 059	35 451	38 607
Dwelling units per household	1.01	1.05	1.08	1.10
Occupied dwelling units	24 198	28 731	32 189	34 705
Vacant housing	1 034	1 720	2 679	3 302
Vacancy ratio (%)	4.0	5.5	7.6	8.6

Source: Ministry of Construction.

the housing supply situation is unsatisfactory. There is, however, a complex interrelationship between the number of households and the number of housing units. This involves such factors as the cost of housing in relation to the income of households and the quality and situation of the vacant units. In Japan one-third of the 3.3M vacant units is of very poor quality and another third is extremely small.

Table 23. **International comparison of housing provision**

	Number of houses per 1 000 persons	Average number of persons per household
Japan	323 (1983)	3.3 (1983)
Denmark	427 (1982)	2.5 (1981)
France	444 (1983)	2.8 (1982)
Germany	438 (1984)	2.4 (1981)
Netherlands	367 (1984)	2.8 (1985)
New Zealand	322 (1983)	3.1 (1981)
Sweden	441 (1980)	2.3 (1980)
United Kingdom	391 (1983)	2.7 (1981)
United States	398 (1981)	2.7 (1980)

Source: OECD Statistics.

The overall housing situation compared with that of other OECD countries (Table 23) shows that in Japan there are about 320 housing units per 1 000 inhabitants, whereas for some Western industrialised countries the number either approaches or even exceeds 400 units. The differences are partly attributable to the comparatively large household size in Japan. But not only is the number of housing units per inhabitant in Japan approximately three-quarters of the level of the housing supply in the best housed OECD countries, the units are typically smaller than housing in these other countries, even though Japanese households are larger. The measure of residential floor space in Japan is the tatami mat (1.7 m^2) and the traditional Japanese life style, which these mats represent, is economical in the use of interior floor space. However, the floor area available per person in Japan – approximately 26 m^2 – is smaller than in a number of OECD countries where the floor area per person is between 35 to 40 m^2.

While household sizes have already fallen considerably in the other countries, this is still occurring in Japan (Table 24). This could aggravate the situation and makes the comparison

Table 24. **Changing household size, 1955-1990**

		1955	1965	1975	1985	1990
Total of ordinary households		17 363	23 085	31 271	38 060	41 060
Household Size	1	601	1 863	4 236	5 694	6 380
	2	1 876	3 292	5 257	7 500	8 633
	3	2 528	4 207	6 259	8 433	9 627
	4	2 890	5 148	8 301	10 261	10 713
	5	2 895	3 733	3 904	3 745	3 430
	6	2 452	2 456	2 037	1 605	1 433
	7	4 140	2 386	1 277	812	644
Average household size		4.97	4.05	3.45	3.19	3.07

Source: Third Comprehensive National Development Plan (Sanzenso), National Land Agency of Japan, 1979.

with other OECD countries of households to housing units potentially more adverse than it is already. Further, there has been a decline in house building rates from a 1972 peak to a current, national production figure of just over 1M units per annum. On the benefit side, falling household size will ease the situation concerning the small size of Japanese housing units, although this may be counteracted by changing life styles.

In 1983, half of the households under the average housing standard and slightly more than half under the minimum housing standard were in the Tokyo and Osaka metropolitan areas. Housing in the metropolitan areas is generally smaller than for the country as a whole (Table 25) and recently, except for owner occupiers building their own housing, floor space for newly completed dwellings has fallen. One-third of houses in the Tokyo metropolitan area are below 39 m^2 in size, another statistic which serves as a surrogate for the generally poorer living conditions in the large cities as opposed to the rest of Japan. Further, this sub-standard housing tends to be occupied by young couples who are likely to leave the large cities if affordable housing is not available.

Table 25. **Housing standards in Japan, 1983**

	No. of rooms per house	Total floor space per house (m^2)
Japan	4.73	85.92
National Capital Metropolitan Area	3.90	66.82
Kinki Metropolitan Area	4.50	74.72

Source: Ministry of Construction.

The housing situation is only approximately illustrated in the average figures for a nation as a whole. Even in countries with a good supply of housing there exist to a smaller or larger degree a skewed distribution. In Japan an indicator of distribution is calculated by the concepts of minimum and average housing standards introduced in 1976. For the minimum housing standard, the gross floor area per person is set at 21 m^2 for one person, 18 m^2 for two person and 16 m^2 for three person households. The units have to be equipped with toilet, washroom, bathroom for the exclusive use of the household (except for single persons). For the average housing standards the gross floor area is about 50 to 70 per cent greater per person (36, 30 and 27m^2 respectively) and the equipment includes heating and hot water supply.

From 1963 to 1983 the improvement of housing conditions has been maintained (Table 26). The share of households below minimum housing standards decreased from 30 to 15 per cent of the total from 1963-78. The corresponding figure for households with below average housing standards decreased from 71 per cent to 58 per cent. However, from 1978 to 1983 this trend continued at a much reduced rate and the share of households living in below minimum standard housing decreased to 11.4 per cent while the corresponding figure for below average standard housing fell to 51 per cent. The 1978 percentages for Japan as a whole were not achieved in the three largest metropolitan areas until 1983.

The housing cost-income ratio may be used as an indicator to illustrate the burden of housing costs. Data on construction costs and disposable income show that recently in Japan the rate of increase is about the same. But, compared with other OECD countries, the cost-income ratio is less favourable. In Japan, it has for the last five years been 4.3 to 5.1 for a condominium and 6.2 to 6.8 for a house. For many households this ratio will be prohibitive in respect of the initial affordability of housing.

Table 26.   **Dwelling size and occupancy in Japan, 1963-1983**

	Year	Total	Owner-occupied housing	Rental housing
Number of rooms per house	1963	3.82	4.56	2.49
	1968	3.84	4.76	2.44
	1973	4.15	5.22	2.60
	1978	4.52	5.65	2.79
	1983	4.73	5.85	2.87
Total floor space per house (m²)	1963	72.52	91.28	38.78
	1968	73.86	97.42	38.05
	1973	77.14	103.09	39.49
	1978	80.28	106.16	40.64
	1983	85.92	111.67	42.88
Number of persons per room	1963	1.16	1.08	1.42
	1968	1.03	0.95	1.29
	1973	0.87	0.79	1.12
	1978	0.77	0.70	0.99
	1983	0.71	0.65	0.91

Source: Ministry of Construction.

D.   Renewal and Renovation

Compared with the encouragement of new building, the priority given to remodelling and rebuilding existing neighbourhoods has been much lower. Housing in these areas consists, to a very large extent, of small units of low quality. The fragmentation of land and leases make land readjustment and renewal projects extremely difficult to implement. Nevertheless, measures do exist to encourage urban renewal. The Urban Development Fund was established in 1966 to provide long-term, low-interest loans to local bodies for land acquisition. The fund is available for acquiring land:

   i)   Occupied by factories and other related facilities in the National Capital and Kinki Regions, where industrial development is restricted;

   ii)   For urban facilities (e.g. roads, parks, sewerage) in the 33 principal cities of Japan; and

   iii)   For urban renewal in the National Capital and Kinki regions.

Recently an increased emphasis has been put on involving private sector initiative and resources in urban renewal schemes. In 1983 MOC introduced a series of measures to this end. Three main approaches, which are principally applicable to Tokyo, have been pursued. The areas covered by zoning for intensive use have been extended; building restrictions have been eased; and public sector land releases have been made.

The legislation for urban renewal is complex with the Building Standards Act, 1950, the Land Readjustment Act, 1954, and the Residential Area Improvement Act, 1974. There are also many types of urban renewal project (Table 27). The following can undertake urban redevelopment projects:

   i)   An individual;

   ii)   An urban redevelopment association;

Table 27. **Types of urban renewal projects in Japan**

Type of Project (Year of Introduction)	Subsidy Rate
Land Readjustment Project (1954)	Project costs when roads of a certain standard or over are built or improved (2/3 or 1/2)
Residential area improvement project (1960)	Deteriorated house purchase and removal (1/2) Public facilities improvement (2/3) Rented improved house construction cost (2/3) Land purchase and formation (2/3) Common facilities, improvement of houses in lots (1/3)
Urban redevelopment project (1969)	Survey, design and planning (1/3) Land improvement (1/3) Common facilities improvement (1/3) Roads (1/2 to 3/5)
Model residential environment improvement project (1978)	Deteriorated house purchase and removal (1/2) Public facilities improvement (1/2) Rented model house construction cost (2/3) Land purchase and formation (1/2) Common facilities, improvement of houses in lots (2/3)
Comprehensive improvement promotion project for residential areas (1979) (Applies in 3 largest metropolitan areas only)	Improvement planning (1/3) Building removal (1/3) Common facilities improvement (1/3) Construction cost of rented houses for current tenants (1/2, 2/3) Public facilities improvement (Subsidies of the same proportion for projects of facilities of the same kind)
Urban non-inflammable building promotion (1980)	Planning (1/3) Non-inflammable building promotion (1/2)
Improvement project for wooden rental housing districts (1982)	Improvement planning expenses (1/2) Building renewal promotion (Expenses for removal, design and common facilities improvement) within a subsidy rate of 1/3 and 1/2 of municipality subsidy Land purchase promotion (1/2) Wooden rented housing improvement (1/2, 1/3)
Co-operative urban housing improvement project (1983)	Survey, design and planning (1/3) Land formation (1/3) Common facilities improvement (only for rented houses [1/3])

iii)   A local government;
iv)   The JHUDC;
v)   The Japan Regional Development Corporation;
vi)   The Metropolitan Expressway Public Corporation;
vii)   The Hanshin Expressway Public Corporation; and
viii)   Local Housing Supply Corporations.

The owner or the leaseholder of housing land within an "effective utilisation district", or a person who obtains their agreement to implement a project, can become an individual executor. An urban redevelopment association is defined as a public corporate entity, composed of the owners or the leaseholders within the project district. But people other than those who hold or control the title of the land can also participate as association members.

The JHUDC can implement projects in order to improve districts where urban renewal should be promoted in a unified and comprehensive manner, in the built-up areas of large cities. The Japan Regional Development Corporation can implement projects in cases where it also prepares land for housing. The Metropolitan and Hanshin Expressway Public Corporations can implement projects in cases where a motorway is being constructed.

However, the main basis for urban renewal in Japan is the Urban Renewal Act, 1969, as revised in 1975 and 1980. The former revision introduced Category II urban redevelopment projects, founded on compulsory public land acquisition, while the latter revision introduced long-term plans for the larger cities (Table 28). Public bodies, such as local governments and JHUDC, carry through projects using legislative powers or budgetary assistance. Also, private sector activity is encouraged by subsidies from JHUDC to urban redevelopment associations. The criteria for implementing an urban renewal project is that two-thirds of the housing lacks fireproofing, the land use pattern is undesirable and that the project will contribute to the more general revival of the area. The average size of scheme is slightly less than 2 hectares.

Table 28. **Plans for urban redevelopment: submission dates**

Sendai	1984	Urawa	1985
Kawasaki	1984	Ohmiya	1985
Yokohama	1984	Tokyo (23 wards)	1985
Nagoya	1984	Tachikawa	1985
Kobe	1985	Chiba	1985
Amagasaki	1985	Funabashi	1985
Nishinomiya	1985	Osaka	1985
Fukuoka	1985	Sakai	1986
Kitakyushu	1985	Higashi Osaka	1986
Sapporo	1985	Hiroshima	1986
Kawaguchi	1985	Kyoto	1986

Source: Ministry of Construction.

Specifically for housing areas, Residential Area Improvement Projects (RAIP) have been prepared since 1960 and, more recently, Model Residential Environment Improvement Projects (MREIP) have been introduced. The latter reflect the move to modernisation and repair as opposed to comprehensive renewal schemes. The criteria for establishing the two designations is as follows:

	HID	MREIP
Minimum size	0.15 hectares	1.0 hectares
Substandard housing	80 %	50 %
Minimum housing density	80 dwellings per hectare	50 dwellings per hectare
Number of substandard houses	50+	50+

There are also some examples of the large-scale redevelopment of existing urban areas, but these follow the general approach to Japanese urban policy, which was not to give priority to the revitalisation of existing urban areas. However, as reflected in the performance of the economy and especially of the housing market, it is doubtful whether it is possible to raise the housing standards of the 4 million households below the minimum standard entirely through new housing construction. The need to improve existing housing in urban areas has been more strongly expressed in recent years and there are a number of comprehensive improvement promotion projects, carried through by local public bodies. However, there is only a small number of projects compared to the volume and complexity of the general urban housing problem. Also, there are HLC promotion programmes for assisting the purchase of second-hand houses.

The annual rate of housing improvement ("housing reform") has recently been approximately 200 000 p.a., a ratio of 1:6 to new housing starts. For HLC loans 13 per cent now go to improvement and there is a 7 000 units per year programme to improve existing publicly operated housing. But these figures are low compared to the high number of small and sub-standard houses. As needs change over time more emphasis will need to be given to renovation.

E. Policy Conclusions

The Japanese government is pursuing a two-pronged approach in its drive for urban improvements. It is promoting decongestion by supporting the development of new towns at selected locations outside (but often closely associated with) existing metropolitan areas and by encouraging alternative sub-centres within the metropolitan areas. At the same time it is increasingly encouraging renewal of the older, overcrowded, inadequately serviced parts of the larger cities. There is a growing appreciation that current programmes, while certainly commendable and in many respects successful, are insufficient to match the speed of deterioration of the quality of life in the larger metropolitan areas. One response to this is an interest in securing an increased level of private investment in urban development and renewal programmes.

Redevelopment rather than restoration is the currently preferred option for improving older urban areas. A comprehensive project is easier to organise and can be implemented in one operation, once agreement and approval is secured. It usually allows too for a more orderly arrangement of streets and sites and for the provision of more open space, for recreational activity as well as disaster relief measures. Despite these advantages a greater emphasis on spontaneous renewal of existing properties on an individual basis could, if given more public sector support, usefully supplement and extend current redevelopment efforts. There is a very strong project approach to urban development in Japan. While the project response achieves speedy and highly visible results, a more exploratory examination of alternatives might suggest less costly and more satisfactory courses of action.

Land readjustment and other measures employed to implement urban redevelopment schemes have tended to produce a somewhat sterile and uninteresting townscape. "Grid-iron" street patterns and site division into rectangular building plots combined with a utilitarian building style may be the least-cost approach, but is generally devoid of variety. More recognition could be given to the animation and intricacy of the existing urban environment, where an inter-mixture of uses creates a vibrant atmosphere and a strong feeling of community inter-dependence. Redevelopment and renewal that combines some of the safety and efficiency of the new with the interest and variety of the old should be encouraged.

Production targets in recent housing programmes have not been achieved because demand did not reach the expected level and household formation rates were lower than predicted. To a substantial degree housing demand in Japan relies on low-interest, long-term loans, which are not responsive to alterations in the overall economic situation. To fulfill policies which increase spending on housing to stimulate domestic demand, increasing diversity is needed in housing finance policies.

The goals set in the 1981-85 housing programme are aimed to ensure that, by 1986, no household would live in accommodation below the minimum housing standards. The overall economic development of Japan and the lack of policy priority and investment for housing have led to a slowdown in housing construction. In the light of the relatively low housing supply in Japan compared with other OECD countries, much higher priority needs to be devoted to housing if the Japanese housing supply is to be substantially improved. This is despite the fact that, measured by the relation between investment in housing to GDP, the performance of Japan compared with other OECD countries is favourable.

To maintain the demand for improved housing, the system of subsidies may need to be further reorientated to assist households during the initial years of house purchase. This would enable current private housing targets to be reached and for domestic demand to be boosted. The conditions of the most poorly housed sections of the population could be improved by putting more emphasis on the remodelling and repair of existing housing areas. The basis of housing policies should be further widened, to take into account urban environmental improvement and revitalisation considerations and to attract self-help resources. Also, the loss of population from inner urban areas of the larger cities would be reduced if more emphasis was given to improving older neighbourhoods.

In view of the importance of disaster reduction measures, considered later, a more sustained effort needs to be put into remodelling older areas and extending fire resistance treatment of existing buildings. Model schemes of low-rise high-density housing, as opposed to the recent stress on high rise schemes, should be encouraged to test their suitability in Japanese cities. These schemes should give more recognition to the qualities of variety and vitality found in the older areas of Japanese cities and more use should be made of traditional Japanese architectural styles and motifs.

Chapter 6

PROVISION OF URBAN INFRASTRUCTURE

The third objective in the City Planning Act, 1968, against which this examination of urban policy in Japan is being conducted, concerns the promotion of public welfare. This concept can be translated into urban policy terms by an examination of the infrastructure provided to urban residents. The fourth objective of a healthy and cultured urban life similarly depends on the level of urban infrastructure and service provision.

Consideration of urban infrastructure provision is also closely interrelated with the chapters on balanced development and the rational use of land, in which infrastructure provision is an important component, and housing and urban environmental standards, to which infrastructure provision makes an important contribution. To keep the topic within reasonable limits, four types of infrastructure need – Road Transport, Sewerage and Water Supply, Urban Parks and Disaster Reduction – which are particularly relevant to future urban policies in Japan, have been selected for examination. There then follows, in the next chapter, an examination of finance for infrastructure.

Although Japan's cities are long established, their stock of public infrastructure is not. Following large scale destruction many cities were rebuilt in a short period after 1945. In a crisis situation opportunities were not taken to provide modern infrastructure and to adopt layouts which favoured the improvement of amenities and anti-disaster measures. This period of rebuilding was followed, as has been shown, by one of rapid urbanisation. Considering the challenges created by these trends, infrastructure provision in the post-war period has generally been consistently pursued in Japan (Table 29). In the 1970s expenditure increased threefold. In the same period, while spending on disaster prevention stayed level at approximately 5 per cent of GDP, expenditure on roads was cut severely, but still remains at a high level.

Table 29. **Public infrastructure provision, 1960-1983**

	1960	1965	1970	1975	1980	1983
Length of urban motorways (km)	–	39	164	199	286	329
Paving of municipal roads (%)	1.5	4.4	12.0	27.0	41.0	49.4
Sewerage diffusion rate (%)	6	8	14	23	28	33
Improvement of urban roads (%)	19	26	27	32	36	39
Improvement of major rivers (%)	40	42	46	51	57	59
Urban parks (m²/person)	2.1	2.4	2.7	3.4	4.1	4.7
Steep slope failure prevention works (%)	–	–	0.3	2.4	9.6	14.1

Source: Ministry of Construction.

The urban capital stock that has been provided in Japan is, therefore, much newer and has been provided more rapidly than in other economically advanced countries. However, much remains to be achieved to improve the welfare of Japanese urban dwellers. Also, the costs for the provision of infrastructure after development has taken place, have been shown to rise by a factor of four. Urban growth has proceeded more rapidly than the supply of public urban services. As shown in Chapter 2, private investment and consumption have been relatively favoured at the expense of public investment and consumption, and rates of infrastructure provision compare unfavourably with other OECD countries (Table 30). This relative lack of infrastructure in Japan tends to be an urban phenomenon, although for sewerage provision the very large cities have a higher level of provision than elsewhere.

Table 30. **Level of infrastructure provision, selected OECD countries**

	Japan	Germany	United Kingdom	United States
Sewerage diffusion rate	34	89	98	72
	(1985)	(1979)	(1981)	(1977)
Motorways (km/1 000 cars)	8.3	31.5	15.5	43.1
	(1985)	(1983)	(1983)	(1980)
Housing (persons per room)	0.74	0.6	0.65	0.6
	(1980)	(1981)	(1981)	(1980)
Area of Park per person (m^2)	(Tokyo)	(Bonn)	(Londres)	(Washington)
	1.9	51.0	33.0	45.7
	(1981)	(1980)	(1981)	(1976)

Source: National Statistics.

Another important issue in this context is the role of infrastructure in economic policy and for economic development. There is, in all OECD countries, a continuous need to balance private and public sector investment. The need to increase and improve the infrastructure in Japanese cities is very clearly recognised and long-range targets, approved by the government and the Diet, have been set up for many fields of infrastructure. But the means have not been forthcoming to realise these long-range targets, as shown in the sections to follow on specific types of infrastructure. Further, although not a priority issue at the present time because most urban infrastructure is relatively new, there will be increasing calls for maintenance and replacement of infrastructure as the stock ages. This will compete with resources for new investment if spending levels are not increased.

A. Road Transport

The high densities of Japanese cities and their rapid growth when traffic demands were much lower than today has created many difficulties for the creation of an efficient, safe and environmentally acceptable system of communications in urban areas. To overcome these difficulties the provision of urban traffic facilities has been actively pursued, especially the development of suburban railway systems, many of them privately owned. The underground railway systems in the larger cities are particularly efficient and, together with the public and private railways and the bus network, provide comprehensive urban public transport systems.

Map 6

URBAN MOTORWAYS IN TOKYO
(As of April 1983)

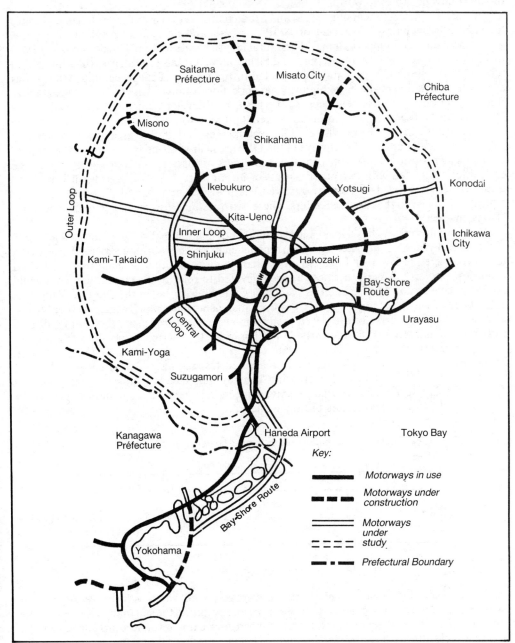

Source: *Ministry of Construction*

The national railway makes very considerable losses but the reasons lie in the rural not the urban parts of the network. In technical and functional terms Japanese urban transportation systems, for example the Tokyo metro and the Portliner guideway system in Kobe, are among the most advanced in the world.

The recent development of national and urban motorways is impressive. Japan continues to spend approximately 2 per cent of GDP on roads and an extensive system of central government financial support applies. Their total length has risen from 239 kilometres in 1965 to 3 536 kilometres in 1982. In international terms, however, this provision is still quite low, in relation to the number of cars and the expected future growth of car ownership. Many cities await the completion of the basic highway network. For example, Tokyo is many years away from having a ring road system because the pattern of development was established before 1960 and the subsequent growth in car ownership (Map 6).

The length of highways where traffic volumes exceed traffic capacity is increasing, accounting for 49 per cent of highways in the DID areas in 1980, an indication of the scale of the challenge still to be met. The congestion and lack of space for circulation reinforces the difficulties associated with two other aspects of urban policy[1]. The first is the disruption to traffic when other infrastructure (e.g. sewers) is provided or repaired. The second is the difficulty of access in the case of disasters. These two questions are considered in later sections of this chapter.

The number of cars has tripled and the number of commercial vehicles doubled in Japan in the past 15 years. As an indication of current deficiencies, the ratio of urban road area to the total urban area is lower in Japanese cities than in cities in other economically advanced countries. In North American cities the area devoted to road traffic circulation is typically 20-25 per cent and in European cities 15-20 per cent, while in Japan the equivalent figure is 5-15 per cent. The use of private cars is, however, increasing more rapidly than in other OECD countries. Although bicycles are a well used form of personal transport, the number of cars rose from 2.3 million in 1965 to nearly 24 million in 1980. Approximately 40 per cent of all passenger transport in Japan is by private car: in 1965 the figure was only 13 per cent. Transportation by bus and railway has decreased correspondingly. This situation has led to increased traffic congestion and decreasing bus running speeds (Table 31). This in turn discourages the use of public transport in cities. In new urban development only 30 per cent of the standard for road provision is usually achieved.

Table 31. **Bus running speeds in three largest cities, 1960-1983**

Km/hr

Cities	1960	1965	1970	1975	1980	1983
Tokyo	15.3	13.6	13.2	12.4	12.0	11.7
Nagoya	16.7	14.9	13.4	13.0	13.0	12.7
Osaka	13.2	11.8	11.8	11.6	11.3	11.3

Of all roads in urban areas only 13 per cent are equipped with pavements. Pedestrians in Japan are, therefore, more exposed to traffic risks and pollution than in many other countries. Although the Japanese record of road safety is good, approximately one-third of people killed in traffic accidents are pedestrians. This figure is being improved, but remains a much higher share than in most other OECD countries. Parking is also difficult in urban centres and causes

Table 32. **Goods vehicles in use, selected OECD countries, 1970-1983**

Thousands

	1970	1975	1980	1981	1982	1983
Japan	8 282	10 044	13 178	13 956	14 717	15 500
Australia	928	1 112	1 452	1 501	1 542	1 550
Denmark	248	228	253	243	236	236
France	2 065	2 325	2 514	2 568	2 695	3 037
Germany	1 028	1 121	1 277	1 307	1 291	1 291
Netherlands	303	332	361	375	377	380
New Zealand	172	207	254	265	281	284
Sweden	145	157	182	186	194	202
United Kingdom	1 630	1 791	1 788	1 763	1 728	1 750
United States	18 797	25 781	33 637	34 894	35 070	35 253

Source: OECD Environmental Data Compendium, 1985.

traffic congestion and consequently higher costs for urban economic activities. This point applies particularly in Japan with its heavy reliance on road transport for the movement of goods (Table 32) and its particularly high levels of urban commuting. The costs of congestion, as well as the wish for improved amenities, has led to the gradual decongestion of large European and North American cities. This trend can be anticipated to accelerate in Japan.

B. Sewerage and Water Supply

Large areas of Japanese cities have been constructed and reconstructed without either sewerage provision or plans for such provision. This is a topic of growing political interest as public opinion surveys show that there is a rising level of concern about the lack of sewerage in cities. The inadequacy of waste water disposal facilities is leading to local environmental problems in residential areas and, more generally, water quality standards for lakes and

Table 33. **Sewerage diffusion rates in Tokyo and designated cities, 1985**

City	Population served (%)
Tokyo	82
Sapporo	92
Kawasaki	51
Yokohama	60
Nagoya	87
Kyoto	74
Osaka	99
Kobe	94
Hiroshima	43
Kitakyushyu	83
Fukuoka	64

Source: Ministry of Construction.

reservoirs are not being achieved, as shown in Chapter 8. Constructing sewerage systems in existing urban areas is expensive and difficult, particularly as densities in Japanese cities are high and land acquisition costly. There are nevertheless considerable differences between cities in Japan concerning sewerage provision (Table 33). The larger the settlement concerned the higher the diffusion rate (Table 34). On average, the coverage of sewerage systems has increased from 8 per cent of the population in 1965 to 34 per cent in 1985. This figure is much lower than in other OECD countries, most of which have rates of 85-90 per cent. The target set by the Government is to achieve such levels in Japan at the beginning of the next century. The financing of sewerage construction is more heavily subsidised than in other OECD countries. This, combined with financial restraints, is probably one of the main reasons for the past delay in sewerage provision, as well as presenting a difficulty in the future for the achievement of the long-range target.

Table 34.   **Sewerage diffusion rates by settlement size, 1985**

City size	Population served (%)
1 m +	78
0.5 m - 1 m	53
0.3 m - 0.5 m	41
- 0.3 m	18
National average	34

Source: Ministry of Construction.

Only three-quarters of the overall target was reached in the recently completed five year plan for sewerage provision. At this rate of progress it would take beyond the end of the century to achieve the dispersion rates in comparable OECD countries. However, where sewerage is provided in the course of land readjustment projects, in which direct costs to the public sector are considerably reduced, 80 per cent of the target was achieved and this is a useful indicator for future policy. Further, although Section 75 of the City Planning Act, 1968, has not been extensively applied, the legal provision that those who have specially benefitted from city planning schemes should contribute to them has been used in the case of sewerage schemes.

Rainfall levels in Japan are comparatively high, which explains the rice-growing basis of Japanese culture. However, alongside the risks of flood which are considered later, there are

Table 35.   **Recent major water shortages in Japanese cities**

Year	City	Duration of water supply restriction	Main river
1977/8	Yodo river plain cities	134 (days)	Yodo River
"	Naha and neighbouring cities	176	–
1978/9	Fukuoka	287	Chikugo River
"	Yodo river plain cities	159	Yodo River
"	Kitakyushu	173	Onga River
1981/2	Naha and neighbouring cities	326	–

Source: Ministry of Construction.

also water shortages. The creation of water supply sources is another area of infrastructure provision which is falling behind demand. Major water shortages are common and the areas affected widespread (Table 35). Also under this heading, river management is an important urban policy issue in Japan, particularly in the light of the rapid urbanisation of the flat alluvial coastal areas in the last 40 years. The main reasons for this are:

   i)   The considerable percentage of the population living in areas where flood control measures are needed for safety reasons (Table 36);

   ii) The importance of rivers for water supply; and

   iii) Environmental considerations.

All three aspects of water control raise questions about the effectiveness of current infrastructure policies.

Table 36. **Flood risks in Japan**

	1960		1970		1980	
Population in areas susceptible to flood (%)	41.7 m	(44.7)	48.0 m	(46.3)	56.4 m	(48.2)
Assets in areas susceptible to flood[1](%)	62	(51)	196	(63)	427	(72)

1. Trillion Yen at 1980 prices.
Source: Ministry of Construction.

Domestic water consumption in Japanese cities is as high, in some cases even higher, than in many European cities and the price is also higher. The development of water resources has been delayed in some urban areas and water shortages are occurring and are expected to occur in the two largest metropolitan areas by 1990. The situation is being further aggravated as urbanisation continues.

C.   Urban Parks and Open Space

The concept of a public urban park is of recent origin in Japan, dating back just over a century to a Cabinet decision of 1873. However, recent efforts to improve the standard of open space provision in Japanese cities is based on the City Parks Act, 1956. Even so it took 16 years to formulate the first five-year programme for parks provision, commencing in 1972 (Table 37). Since that date spending has risen slowly in subsequent five year programmes and

Table 37. **Provision of city parks, 1972-1985**

	1st programme (1972-76)		2nd programme (1976-80)		3rd programme[1] (1981-85)	
	Planned	Implemented	Planned	Implemented	Planned	Implemented
Total Investment (Y100M)	9 000	5 728	16 500	15 960	28 800	20 214
Area (hectares)	16 500	8 319	14 400	10 784	12 011	–
		(50.4 %)		(74.9 %)		
Area per capita (m²/person)	2.8 - 4.2	3.4	3.4 - 4.5	4.1	4.1 - 5.0	4.9

1. Estimate: 1981-4 + 1985 budget.
Source: Ministry of Construction.

currently stands at 0.2 per cent of GDP. In April 1981 a higher profile was given to this topic by the establishment of the Urban Green Space Development Foundation, a public body supported by voluntary contributions.

The increase in leisure time; the rising percentage of elderly people in Japanese cities; and the value of open space in disaster reduction measures, discussed in the next section, have given added reasons for the provision of urban parks. However, it was the Emergency Measures for Developing City Parks Act, 1972, which provided the impetus lacking in previous legislation to formulate the first five year programme referred to above.

Table 38. **Park provision rates by city size, 1973-1983**

M² person

City size	1973	1978	1983
1 m +	2.1	2.7	3.5
0.5 m - 1 m	3.0	4.0	4.7
0.3 m - 0.5 m	3.4	4.2	5.2
0.3 m	3.3	4.1	5.1

Source: Ministry of Construction.

Table 39. **Parks in Tokyo and designated cities 1971-1981**

M²/person

City	1971	1981
Tokyo (23 wards)	1.23	2.01
Sapporo	3.27	5.22
Kawasaki	1.15	3.32
Yokohama	2.61	1.99
Nagoya	3.32	4.37
Kyoto	1.50	2.33
Osaka	1.67	2.48
Kobe	2.88	6.58
Hiroshima	–	5.36
Kitakyushu	3.13	6.54
Fukuoka	2.58	4.83
Average	1.86	3.24

Source: Ministry of Construction.

The per capita size of parks in the largest Japanese cities is 3.5 m², a much lower figure than in smaller cities (Tables 38 and 39). In Tokyo the figure is 2 m² per person, which can be compared with 46 m² in Washington, 33 m² in London, 10 m² in Paris and 80 m² in Stockholm (Table 40). The long-term target for City Parks in Japan is 20 m² per person at the beginning of the 21st century. In this light the rate of progress in the five year plans will need to be considerably increased. The situation is more unsatisfactory than it might seem because at the same time as parks are being provided at a slow rate, other open space is disappearing

Table 40. **Parks in selected OECD capital cities**

City	Area of park (ha)	Per capita (m²)	Year
Tokyo	1 688	2	1982
Amsterdam	1 052	15	1983
Copenhagen	803	14	1981
London	21 828	33	1981
Paris	2 246	10	1982
Stockholm	5 300	80	1976
Washington	3 458	46	1976
Wellington	2 037	151	1981

Source: OECD.

Table 41. **Green space conservation zones, 1966-1981**

Year	Number of cities	Number of zones	Size (ha)
1966	3	3	129.0
1971	7	11	964.4
1976	21	69	1 506.1
1981	24	129	1 722.5

Source: Ministry of Construction.

quickly. In Tokyo, woodland has been reduced from 11 per cent to 3 per cent of the total area in the last 40 years, while the area of parks has stayed at approximately 3 per cent.

Although severely affected by rising land prices, which make the acquisition of land for parks a major constraint, the area of urban parks has been doubled in the last decade. It is intended that 30 per cent of Urban Promotion Areas should be designated for open space, but as yet progress has been very slow (Table 41). For example, in the Tokyo metropolitan area only 82 hectares have been designated under the Urban Green Space Conservation Act, 1973. As mentioned in Chapter 3, it was on this point that the 1958 plan for Tokyo failed. The plan contained proposals for a Green Belt, however opposition from land owners ensured that the plan proposals were not adopted. A clear opportunity to structure the development of the Tokyo Metropolitan Area around proposals for the adequate provision of open space was missed.

D. Disaster Reduction

Several major disasters, such as earthquakes, fires, typhoons and floods cause widespread loss of life and property in Japan (Table 42). 10 per cent of the world's earthquakes are recorded in Japan and there is, therefore, a high degree of concern over the continuing vulnerability of overcrowded, densely populated cities, which has increased as the urban population has risen. The situation has been aggravated by the scale of recent urbanisation leading to higher buildings and the use of less suitable land. The increasing sophistication of city services also increases the vulnerability to disasters. In Japan many

Table 42.   **Major natural disasters of geological origin, OECD countries, 1975-1983**

	Location	Type of disaster	Fatalities
1975	Japan	Landslide	30
	Turkey	Earthquake	2 300
1976	Italy	Earthquake	1 000
	Japan	Landslide	35
	Turkey	Earthquake	5 300
1977	Turkey	Earthquake	9
	Greece, Turkey and Bulgaria	Earthquake	50
1978	Japan	Earthquake	25
	Japan	Earthquake	21
	Greece	Earthquake	47
1979	Yugoslavia	Earthquake	100
	Yugoslavia and Albania	Earthquake	200
1980	Portugal	Earthquake	60
	United States	Landslide	36
	Turkey	Landslide	60
	United States	Volcanic	62
	Greece	Earthquake	–
	Japan	Landslide	20
	Italy	Earthquake	3 000
1981	Greece	Earthquake	20
	Portugal	Landslide	26
1982	Italy	Earth Tremors	–
	Italy	Landslide	–
1983	United States	Earthquake	–
	Japan	Tidal Wave	100
	Japan	Landslide	70
	Turkey	Earth Tremors	1 350

Source: OECD Environmental Data Compendium, 1985.

houses are flimsy and highly combustible and are unlikely to su vive a major disaster. Narrow streets, congested housing and the lack of open space, which can provide a firebreak, increase the risks arising from a disaster and makes either prevention or containment much more difficult.

The risk of floods has been described in the section of this chapter on sewerage and water supply. Short, steep rivers are characteristic and water volumes can increase quickly. In the current five year flood control programme half the budget for flood control measures for small and medium rivers is spent in urban areas. Also associated with heavy rainfall is the risk of land slips and slope failures. Subsidies are paid for the relocation of housing from areas of high risk.

Ways of minimising the extent and possible impacts of disasters occupy a prominent place in Japanese urban policy. This need underlies the preference for urban renewal rather than urban renovation, so that a new and improved road network and more generous open space can be provided to secure evacuation routes and safe assembly areas for people who may be displaced or threatened by a disaster. It also explains the current preference in redevelopment schemes for concrete and other fire resistant materials rather than wood. Nevertheless, the number of fire proofed buildings remains limited. In the city of Tokyo more than half the housing remains to be fire proofed and approximately one-fifth of the city presents access difficulties for fire fighting equipment. It has been estimated that an earthquake of the same magnitude as that in the Kanto plain in 1923 would lead to 36 000 casualties in Tokyo, with a third of the city being destroyed.

Considerable efforts have been made over the past twenty years, since the Fire Proof Buildings Promotion Act, 1952, including the Creation of Disaster Prevention Blocks Act, 1961, to minimise the risks of urban fires. Thus, although this aspect of disaster-reduction based urban policy is making progress, much remains to be achieved. As with redevelopment generally, implementation is on a random basis in several locations scattered throughout the metropolitan areas. To achieve more, either redevelopment and renewal schemes will have to be greatly expanded, or more attention will have to be devoted to extending fire resistant treatment of existing buildings. The more effective deployment of and access for the fire and disaster prevention services will also be necessary, as part of gradual renewal policies.

E. Policy Conclusions

Public goods are part of the general welfare of a society and infrastructure and services for urban residents are an important part of social welfare. The stock of urban infrastructure in Japan is relatively small, both in comparison with the national standards that have been set and in international terms. Furthermore, the growth rate regarding investments in infrastructure is decreasing at the same time as the demand for infrastructure and services is increasing. There will be a continuing higher than average need for infrastructure investment in Japan, because of the requirement for disaster prevention and the low level of existing provision. In general, the larger cities and their hinterlands, which had to be rebuilt quickly 40 years ago and have since expanded considerably, have generally lower standards of infrastructure than elsewhere in Japan and will have the greatest future priorities.

Trends which are leading to further urbanisation in Japan, combined with increasing deconcentration in metropolitan areas, will continue to create demand for new urban infrastructure. A point not given as much attention as the question of quantity is the present and future need to maintain and improve the quality of the existing stock of infrastructure. When considerable resources must be used for the continuous expansion of infrastructure networks, there is a risk that the increasing needs for replacement, maintenance and improvement of the existing stock will be neglected. Examples from other OECD countries, where the quantity gaps are much smaller than in Japan, show that infrastructure maintenance and improvement present considerable challenges, especially if the general economic situation remains unchanged. With slower economic growth and restrictions on public capital investment, meeting maintenance and improvement needs becomes even more difficult.

In four specific sectors of infrastructure provision – urban road transport, sewerage and water supply, parks and open space, and disaster reduction – although progress has been made in the past two decades the rate has been extremely slow. The upgrading of standards of urban infrastructure, unless rates of spending increase sharply, will depend on a long-term sustained investment programme. In boosting domestic demand in Japan through the housing sector, as mentioned earlier, this will itself create a demand for infrastructure which will also play a further part in boosting domestic demand.

NOTE AND REFERENCE

1. Japanese Urban Society and its Cultural Context, G. D. Allinson, in *The City in Cultural Context*, J. Agnew, J. Mercer and D. Sopher (Eds.), Allen and Unwin, Boston, 1984.

Chapter 7

FINANCING URBAN INFRASTRUCTURE

The scale of the infrastructure requirements and the priority areas are appreciated in Japan. However, to make any significant impact on the backlog of provision, additional resources will be required. Athough this Report concentrates on urban policy at the national level, finance for the provision of infrastructure cannot be fully understood without consideration being given to local government finance.

A. Local Government Finance

As described in Chapter 2, Japan has a unitary system of government, which means that the local level carries more responsibility than in a federal political system. By international comparative standards local government in Japan is economically staffed and efficiently run[1]. It also has autonomy with respect to its relations with central government. Article 92 of the Constitution provides that "regulations concerning organisation and operations of local public entities shall be fixed by law in accordance with the principle of local autonomy".

In 1983, just over half of government expenditure was accounted for by local government, taking into account transfers from central government, which amounted to 45 per cent. The key point is that expenditure by local government in Japan is more important than in other OECD countries (Table 43). It is significant, however, that the source of much of local government's finance is central government, through both untied and earmarked grants; that central government controls borrowings and provides a whole complex range of subsidies; and that urban development in Japan is greatly affected by expenditure patterns of the large public corporations, which are funded by central government. In addition, a general trend exists towards a heavier reliance on bonds and central government contributions to finance local government spending. The Home Affairs Ministry's control over property tax rates (Y 500 per m^2) and over the issue of local bonds under "temporary" powers (which have been in effect for over 30 years) greatly limits the financial ability of local government.

The most important single source of revenue for local governments are the local taxes, made up as follows:

Prefectures	Municipalities
Enterprise tax (40 %)	Inhabitants tax (50 %)
Inhabitants tax (30 %)	Property tax (30 %)
Car tax (10 %)	Urban planning tax (5 %)
Petrol tax (5 %)	Tobacco tax (4 %)

Table 43. **Government expenditure by level of government, selected OECD countries, 1981**

Percentage

Country	Central government	State government	Local government
Federal Countries			
Australia	50.3	43.2	6.5
Germany	59.2	21.9	18.9
United States	59.7	17.5	22.8
Unitary Countries			
Denmark	42.5		57.5
France	83.8		16.2
Japan	37.2		62.8
Netherlands[1]	69.0		31.0
New Zealand	86.7		13.3
Sweden	56.5		43.5
United Kingdom	71.6		28.4

1. Local government data include Provincial governments.
Source: *Government Finance Statistics Yearbook,* IMF, Washington D.C., 1981 and 1983 Editions.
  Local Public Finance in Japan, Jichi Sogo Center, Tokyo, February 1982.

Another important source of income is the Local Allocation Tax, which accounts for 17 per cent of local revenues. It is calculated as a one-third share of national taxes, giving local and national government a joint interest in the tax base.

As well as their own taxes and allocations from central government, local authority borrowing is an important source of revenue, particularly for urban development purposes. The main method of borrowing is through the issue of bonds and debentures, with the total amount to be raised controlled by central government. The main subscribers to the loans are local banks and government agencies, including the Trust Fund Bureau, the reserve fund of the Special Post Office Life Insurance and funds from local public enterprise financial corporations. When the funds are to be used for large-scale urban projects of community importance, government contributions are made at low interest rates. The borrowing programme of local authorities appears to be based on these low interest public sector contributions, rather than on a full harnessing of private savings.

An aspect of Japanese local taxation of interest to other OECD countries is the city planning tax, which accounts for approximately 5 per cent of city governments' revenues. It is

Table 44. **City planning tax, 1966-1983**

	Municipalities with city planning projects	Municipalities collecting city planning tax	Amount of city planning tax[1] (A)	Cost of city planning projects (B)	A/B (%)
1966	964	607	23 685	290 233	8.2
1971	1 109	671	95 148	908 531	10.1
1976	1 278	715	224 327	1 804 814	12.4
1981	1 418	776	500 491	3 763 377	13.3
1983	1 459	781	623 482	3 811 728	16.4

1. Million Yen.
Source: Ministry of Construction.

based, with a 0.3 % ceiling, on fixed assets in UPAs and represents a growing source of income for urban development and land readjustment projects (Table 44). As a way of boosting local government revenues, the City of Kobe has shown that, using the existing legislative framework in Japan, it is possible to raise private sector money for infrastructure investment[2]. Four methods have been used:

i) A profits tax, which has a range of 12.3 per cent to 14.7 per cent, available to local governments under the Local Government Taxation Act, 1950;

ii) An informal system of planning gain, to supplement Section 75 of the City Planning Act, 1968, which is only available for expenditure on sewerage;

iii) Public land banking on the basis of a continuing programme; and

iv) The establishment of public development corporations, under the Local Public Enterprise Act, 1952, which borrow from the private banking system to overcome restrictions on the issue of public bonds.

B. Central Government Finance

The success of the Japanese economy in adjusting to the slowdown in world economic activity was described in Chapter 2. Inflation is low; exports are high; the trade balance is very favourable; and real disposable income is rising. However, there is a substantial outflow of long-term capital; there are questions about the effects of the internationalisation of the yen; and concern about the size of public sector debt. This occurs at a time when expectations from the public with respect to infrastructure provision are growing.

As the 1983/84 OECD Economic Survey indicates "the main structural factors behind the rapid rise in expenditure during the 1970s are likely to persist during the next decade or so. There is still a large unsatisfied demand for social capital investment, though the pace of investment may slacken somewhat"[3]. Urban development is closely linked with the national economy and the real challenge for urban policies is to demonstrate that they can contribute to economic growth and assist the process of economic restructuring.

Japan continues to have one of the highest savings ratios in the world. A basic economic policy question is where to draw the line between either retaining private savings for reinvestment in industrial development, aimed at export markets, or providing for an increase in standards of social capital and housing, thereby increasing domestic demand. These wider considerations of economic policy go beyond the scope of an urban review. However, without sustained investment in infrastructure and amenities, it can be said that living conditions in Japanese cities will not improve greatly in the next decade (Diagram 9).

In Japan not only, as was shown in Chapter 2, is the size of the public sector smaller than elsewhere, but the contribution of taxes to government revenues is also low (Table 45).

Table 45. **Ratio of tax revenue to national expenditure 1973-1980**

	1973	1975	1980
Japan	90.4	65.9	61.9
France	93.1	81.4	89.9[1]
Germany	91.6	76.1	82.4
United Kingdom	91.3	83.4	82.6
United States	97.3	80.1	89.1

1. Estimated.
Source: OECD Economic Outlook, 1985.

Diagram 9

PROSPECTS FOR INFRASTRUCTURE INVESTMENT, 1980-2000[1]

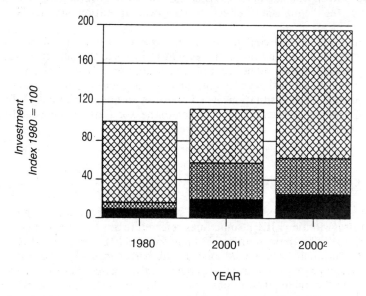

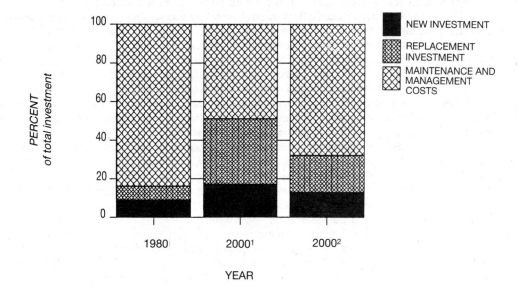

Notes: *Assumptions used to forecast investment in the year 2000:*

1.   *Zero growth of public investment in new and replacement investment;*

2.   *Annual growth of 3 % in new and in replacement investment.*

Source: *National Land Agency.*

However, given the size of the current national deficit, current world uncertainties and an effective ceiling on local borrowings, any urban improvement programme needs to be seen in a long-term perspective. Given the heavy responsibilities of local governments for urban development generally, the "equalising" effect of the local allocation tax needs to be examined.

When there are major financial constraints, providing central government finance to projects unrelated to defined needs and programmes tends to reduce the efficiency of these programmes. In 1983, approximately 60 per cent of expenditure on urban development and infrastructure was financed by central government, making this sector vulnerable to cuts in national public expenditure. In this situation, it is important to finance the most effective projects on the basis of need, by giving priority attention to the worst urban living conditions. These tend to be in the three largest metropolitan areas.

C. Fiscal Investment and Loan Programme

One of the most important revenue sources for infrastructure provision is the Fiscal Investment and Loan Programme (FILP), sometimes referred to as "the second budget" of the Japanese Government. The main sources of funds for the FILP are Postal Savings, Pension Funds and Government guaranteed bonds and borrowings. All are, in effect, individuals' savings deposited with the government. There are two classes of institutions which qualify for these funds: the "financing institutions" such as the Japan Development Bank and the Housing Loan Corporation; and the "Public Corporations" such as the Housing and Urban Development Corporation and the Japan Highway Public Corporation.

The FILP has been successfully used by the Japanese Government as a resource allocation mechanism to meet changing national needs. During the period from 1945 to 1955 resources were diverted to economic recovery through the stimulation of coal mining, electricity generation and the iron and steel industry. From 1955 to 1965 more emphasis was placed on financing new industries and on transport and communications. From 1965 to 1973 the main targets were housing, small and medium sized enterprises and trade promotion. Since the 1973 oil crisis the emphasis has further shifted to housing and other public services, with quality of life considerations becoming more important. In the 1970s, investments in both health care and highways have been made through the FILP.

FILP is well suited to the implementation of urban policy. Central government has a number of other policy instruments that it can use to meet urban policy objectives, including direct involvement in public works; financing local government expenditure; and influence on the tax system. But the FILP has a number of special qualities: it is a loan programme; it is a flexible and targetted programme; it can support public/private sector co-operation; and it ensures an efficient use of public money.

Looking towards the future, the main source of funds for the FILP, especially postal savings, are unlikely to grow at the same rate as in previous periods of high economic growth. Moreover, as the Japanese financial system becomes more liberalised, new types of investment opportunities are becoming available. A greater dependence on bond issues, increasing private finance, or more likely a measure of the two, will be the only way to sustain infrastructure investment. The end result of this combination of economic circumstances is likely to be greater pressure on the government for carefully directed and co-ordinated investment to meet national priorities. These will inevitably include improving the quality of life in urban areas.

D. Sources of Additional Finance

Whether or not the current, restrictive fiscal stance of the Japanese Government is maintained, more funds for urban infrastructure investment need to be sought from other sources. There are three ways to finance future expenditure on urban infrastructure which are not mutually exclusive and can be used in combination with each other and with government expenditure:

- *i)* Private sector provision, either alone or in co-operation with the public sector through the "third" sector;
- *ii)* User charges; and
- *iii)* Direct contributions from developers.

As shown in Chapter 2, there are high levels of borrowing in Japan by both central and local governments. At the same time there are high levels of personal savings and obvious economic success by enterprises engaged in export industries. These circumstances suggest that a greater involvement of the private sector in urban development projects is appropriate. While there are examples of public/private sector co-operation in Japan, a good deal more could be done in this area. This has major implications for future levels of expenditure and investment relative to needs, demands and expectations. It will entail, among other things, new ways of involving private finance in the provision of public services and infrastructure through:

- *i)* Beneficiary taxation and capital cost contributions;
- *ii)* New forms of public/private co-operation in joint financing schemes; and
- *iii)* Privatisation of services and facilities.

This would contribute to domestic demand "by reforming Japan's domestic utilities to enable the private sector to undertake infrastructure investments in place of the fiscally contained public sector"[4].

An example of co-operation for urban development between the public and private sectors is the Japan Project Industry Council (JAPIC). The Ministry of International Trade and Industry and the Ministry of Construction participate, but the membership is primarily from private sector firms in the construction industry. The standard form of promoting large-scale development in Japan has been through public sector corporations, but it is felt that more use should be made of private sector "know-how" in formulating and presenting infrastructure projects, as well as in their construction and management[5].

While the responsibility for major infrastructure investments rests mainly on the central government (Table 46), the responsibility for pricing the use of infrastructure rests mainly on local governments. Coming to the future challenge of maintaining the existing infrastructure stock, another argument arises for alternative pricing systems. If the future maintenance and improvement needs are not covered by user charges, they must be met by government expenditure. So, increased user charges would have two effects: to contribute to increased provision and to create resources for maintenance and replacement of infrastructure facilities.

As regards borrowing for infrastructure investment purposes, there are interesting differences between cities[6]. In Osaka and Kobe the use of local bonds for sewerage investments has been more extensive than in other cities. Consequently, the sewerage provision in these cities is ahead of most other cities in Japan. In Kobe City the great improvement of sewerage provision was accomplished through the extensive use of bond issues

Table 46. **Central government contribution to urban infrastructure provision**

Type of project	Central government contribution
Public sewerage	3/5-2/3
Regional sewerage	3/5-3/4
Urban sewerage	2/5
Sewerage (industry)	2/9-1/4
Sewerage (environmental)	3/5-2/3
Urban parks	1/3-1/2
Green space preservation	1/3-2/3
Urban roads	1/2-2/3
Land readjustment	1/2
Urban redevelopment	1/2-2/3

Source: Ministry of Construction.

to support the standard system of finance. The idea of "community bonds" for improving local infrastructure is the type of innovation which needs to be introduced to build on that experience.

E. Policy Conclusions

As part of its economic policy, the government has established a tentative objective to lower the ratio of bond issues to expenditure and not to depend on deficit financing bonds after FY 1990. It is intended to keep public works bond issues to the 1985/6 level of approximately Y 6 000 billion for the rest of the decade. However, if infrastructure investment is held steady in real terms, an increase in maintenance and replacement costs would limit new investment. A 3 per cent increase, which would have limited effect in the context of the comparatively small size of the public sector in Japan, would dramatically change the situation. This increase would need to come from the combined resources of central and local government, as well as the private sector.

Local government spending is more important in Japan than elsewhere in the OECD area, but local resources come in large measure from the national government. In a period of fiscal and financial restraint it is vital to target infrastructure spending to priority areas. One approach by the national government would be to reflect specific urban needs to a greater extent in allocating funds to local government. Secondly, more use could be made of the Fiscal Investment and Loan Programme to finance priority infrastructure spending. This would be in line with the Japanese Government's programme of stimulating domestic demand.

However, in view of the failure of past rates of infrastructure provision to keep up with short and long-term targets, more private resources will need to be devoted to investment in infrastructure. The means exists in Japan to bring this situation about without new legislation. In financing infrastructure and urban services there should be less emphasis on central government subventions, for both providers and users, and more emphasis on charges for use. Rises in land prices through infrastructure provision, particularly roads, should be recouped to pay for the facilities concerned. Also, more use should be made of procedures which secure infrastructure provision at no public cost, when it is provided by the developers of a project.

As the stock of existing urban infrastructure in Japan has rapidly increased in the last 40 years, more resources will need to be made available for modernisation and maintenance. Central government expenditure on urban development and allocations to local government and public agencies should be more targetted on the basis of need, particularly to the three largest urban areas. To increase the general effectiveness of public investment, there should be better co-ordination of public expenditure on infrastructure provision and upgrading. In particular, the possibility of cross subsidies between new, profitable forms of infrastructure and other infrastructure, where direct charging is less easy, should be considered.

NOTES AND REFERENCES

1. Public Sector Productivity and Work Force Management in Japan, C. Bingham, *Urban Innovation Abroad*, November 1984.
2. *Management of Urban Development*, T. Miyazaki, Kobe City Council, 1985.
3. *Economic Surveys 1982/3: Japan*, OECD, Paris, 1984.
4. How Japan can Import More, *Financial Times*, 1st August 1985.
5. *Present State and Problems of the Public-Private Co-operation in Japanese Urban Development*, S. Ishihara, Tokyo, 1983.
6. *Financial Problems of Japan's Great Cities*, H. Hirooka, United Nations Centre, Nagoya, 1980.

Chapter 8

THE ENVIRONMENT IN URBAN AREAS

The thread that links together the policy issues which have been analysed in previous chapters is a concern with the quality of life in urban Japan. However, there are also a set of policies which immediately address the standard of the urban environment. These relate both to the public welfare and the health and cultural objectives of urban policy referred to in Chapter 1.

A. Urban Amenity and Design

The word "amenity" is used in a variety of contexts. It applies properly to the often optional and less site-specific characteristics and qualities of an area, which contribute to the pleasantness, harmony and coherence of the environment. It is in these respects that many parts of the Japanese metropolitan areas are deficient. There are a few magnificent castles, as at Himeji, water features such as at Yanagawa, and many small parks and shrines of a formal nature. Environmental improvement schemes associated with riverside areas have also been actively promoted, for example, the Sendaihori River in Tokyo and the Hirose River in Sendai City.

But generally the separation of traffic and pedestrian movement, the creation of parks, the availability and design of street furniture, the control of outdoor advertising and the provision for active recreation (both indoor and outdoor), falls short of standards reached in many OECD countries. Urban conservation schemes are also rare, although the recent scheme to conserve Asuka village and the landscape of Kyoto form a basis for developing this aspect of urban policy. However, to date only five "Urban Aesthetic Districts" have been designated, although 36 Special Preservation Districts for Historic Landscapes have been selected under the Special Measures for the Preservation of Historic Landscapes Act, 1966.

Urban sprawl and examples of poorly maintained buildings, untidy vacant sites and the raft of wirescape, that characterises so many residential and commercial areas, constitute another important challenge that needs the attention of public policy makers. Public opinion would favour changes (Table 47). In some prefectures and cities efforts are being made to tackle this urban neglect and to create more green areas, with extensive planting programmes enlisting the support and direct participation of the community. Each year an "Environmental Beautification Activity Day" provides a focus for these activities.

Certainly, public attitudes in Japan seem to have changed from concerns with preventing pollution to more positive attitudes of conservation. In the growing competition between cities to retain and attract residents and enterprises, improving the quality of the urban environment

Table 47.   **Public opinion survey on urban amenities**

Do you agreee with this view?
Although it would cost more, should public authorities pay more attention
to the better design of social facilities?

Percentage

	Number of sample	Yes	No	Don't know	Total
Total	2 404	44	31	25	100
Male	1 098	49	31	20	100
Female	1 306	40	30	30	100
Age					
20-29	352	47	29	24	100
30-39	583	47	31	22	100
40-49	542	45	32	23	100
50-59	452	43	32	25	100
Over 60	475	39	27	34	100

Source: Ministry of Construction.

has emerged as an important policy priority. In the central areas of Japanese cities where very large numbers of people congregate for employment, shopping and recreation, the quality of the urban environment is particularly important. Because of the difficult sub-soil strata, the frequency of earthquake movement and absolute height controls, imposed by city administrations until floor area ratios were introduced, high rise commercial development was not as common in Tokyo and other Japanese cities as in other OECD countries. However, with modern engineering design and a relaxation of height control regulations, the construction of high rise office blocks is increasing.

Whether this increased intensity of use will have commensurate public benefits deserves some consideration. It may be advisable either to require development consent to be conditional on the provision of associated public amenities, or to levy higher charges to support a fund from which such amenities can be provided by the responsible municipality. For example, favourable planning consents can be granted to schemes which include substantial open space provision. Care will have to be taken to ensure that high rise site developments do not seriously degrade neighbouring areas through overshadowing, increases in traffic congestion and a build-up in wind velocities. Winds can be strong at certain times of the year in Japan and the introduction of wind model and other tests would be valuable in considering the design of tall buildings.

High rise residential apartments figure prominently in current redevelopment schemes and in some parts of the new towns. European and American experience has in recent years begun to demonstrate the unsuitability and unpopularity of such residential environments (particularly for families). High rise residential building will always have a part in high density urban living: Hong Kong and Singapore are other Asian examples. In the current housing situation, the improved accommodation will be more than acceptable, but the maintenance and management costs need to be counted as well.

It would be desirable to experiment more with apartments of three or four storeys, thus ensuring a more human scale of development. The cost of such development might well be less and, given careful design, densities could be almost the same. More variety in terms of low-rise high density housing development with a greater use of indigenous and sympathetic building materials would assist the maintenance of a Japanese style of architecture.

The current Japanese government examination of controls and regulations, to see which can be reduced in order to encourage more private investment in urban development, parallels similar moves elsewhere. This approach needs to be examined with caution in Japan, where the achievement of acceptable urban living conditions still requires the upgrading of standards.

B. Environmental Quality

In towns and cities environmental quality considerations go beyond aesthetics and amenity to take into account more measurable parameters, such as air and water quality and noise. With a long tradition of high density urban living, the Japanese people have in the past put considerable store on these aspects of the urban environment. However, these considerations were not taken into great account in the rebuilding and expansion of both Japanese cities and the Japanese economy in the 1950s and 1960s. The cumulative effect of rapid industrialisation and urbanisation, linked to a number of serious environmental disasters, led to a change of public attitudes in the late 1960s and early 1970s, which has grown and developed since. The City Planning Act, 1968, passed the year after the Environmental Pollution Control Act, contains clauses concerning city plans conforming with environmental pollution control plans and for the Environment Agency to be consulted on UPA designations.

The first major legislation to be enacted was the Basic Law for Environmental Pollution Control, 1967. However, it was not until a special session of the Japanese Diet, held on the Environment in 1970, that detailed legislation was passed in the form of 14 environmental pollution control laws. The next year saw the establishment of the Environment Agency, as part of the office of the Prime Minister.

Under the 1967 Act, regular annual reports on the State of the Environment are produced and comprehensive programmes have been formulated for particular areas. Since 1982/3 attention has been given to a third generation of regional pollution control programmes, which include the major cities where anti-pollution measures are now of greatest priority. Governmental funding, including that from the Environmental Pollution Control Service Corporation and the Japan Development Bank, has been provided in the form of loans to industrial companies.

A recent development was the Cabinet decision in 1984 to introduce Environmental Impact Assessment. This will assist a comprehensive approach to environmental quality and the integration of urban and environmental policies. Major new transport facilities, housing and development by Corporations established by special legislation will be subject to EIA, together with designated schemes under the following laws:

New Residential Site Development Project
National Capital Region Development
Development of the Basis of New Cities
Development of Suburban Development and Redevelopment Areas
Land Readjustment
Kinki Region Development
River

While this move is to be welcomed, as experience is gained with operating EIA procedures consideration should be given to an extension to cover a wide range of major schemes by the private sector. The MOC has issued a proclamation specifically calling for environmental considerations to be taken into account in preparing City Plans. Several local governments, for example in Fukuoka, Hokkaido, Tokyo and Kanagawa Prefectures, are also introducing their own EIA requirements.

C. Pollution Problems

In the examination of Environmental Policies in Japan, published in 1977[1], the OECD reviewed the implementation of this new legislation and administrative apparatus. By setting strict ambient standards at national level, backed up by emission standards set by local government, Japan had managed to move from being one of the most polluted countries to one which compared favourably with other OECD countries. High levels of spending on pollution control continue (Table 48). The costs have been largely met by private industry and this has not led to a decline in productivity, an argument often used in other countries by those opposed to investing in anti-pollution measures.

Table 48. **Pollution control expenditures: annual investment by industry, selected OECD countries, 1970-1983**
Index (100 in 1980)

Year	Japan	France	Germany	Netherlands	USA
1970	93	–	–	–	–
1975	320	98	120	78	99
1980	100	100	100	100	100
1983	135	84	–	–	–
% of GDP 1980	0.17%	0.18%	0.23%	0.19%	0.63%

Source: OECD Environmental Data Compendium, 1985.

In terms of the air quality of urban areas, sulphur dioxide and carbon monoxide levels meet the standards. But nitrogen dioxide standards are not reached in many cases, particularly in the three largest metropolitan areas (Table 49). There is an extensive system of air quality monitoring stations (Map 7) and alerts for hazardous levels of photochemical smog occur approximately 10 times per annum. This rate, which had fallen steadily through the 1970s, has risen again recently.

The previous chapters on infrastructure put the stress on sewerage provision, which is directly relevant to environmental improvement: over half the budget for environmental

Table 49. **Concentration of NO$_2$, selected cities, 1970-1983**

	NO$_2$ relative concentration (%)					1975 base reference (ug/m^3)
	1970	1975	1980	1981	1983	
Tokyo	64%	100%	83%	77%	77%	79.6
Kawasaki	94%	100%	76%	76%	90%	65.1
Kanawawa	–	100%	87%	77%	74%	30.0
Nonodake	–	–	100%	200%	200%	2.0

Source: OECD Environmental Data Compendium, 1985.

Map 7

NATIONAL AIR QUALITY MONITORING NETWORK

Nopporo

Sapporo

Nonodake

Sendai

Niigata

Niitsu

Tsukuba

Kashima

Tokyo

Inuyama

Kawasaki

Ichikawa

Matsue

Kyoto

Nagoya

Amagasaki

Kurashiki

Osaka

Kitakyushu

Ube

Kurahashi jima

Chikugo Ogori

Omuta

- ● Air pollution monitoring station

- ∆ Environmental background air monitoring station

protection is spent on sewer construction. The quality of inland waters, particularly urban rivers, is an area of concern for those seeking to improve the standards, particularly of drinking water, in Japanese cities. While four-fifths of sea water samples and two-thirds of river samples meet standards, the proportion falls to two-fifths for lakes and reservoirs.

Previous pollution problems caused by heavy metals have been reduced and organic substances are now the major pollutant. The main source is the discharge of untreated waste water, caused by the delay in installing sewerage in older housing areas and the low overall rate of dispersion of sewerage in Japan, a matter taken up in the chapter on infrastructure provision. Apart from a major effort in the provision of sewers and sewage treatment facilities, no great improvement can be expected in the quality of inland water in urban Japan[2]. The degree of sewerage provision in Japan is low compared with other OECD countries (Table 50) and the eutrophication of Lake Biwa (Table 51) and the infamous "red tides" of Tokyo Bay are witness to this state of affairs.

Table 50. **Population served by waste water treatment plants, selected OECD countries, 1970-1983**

Percentage

	1970	1975	1980	1983
Japan	16.0	23.0	30.0	33.0
Denmark	54.3	70.6	–	90.0
France	–	40.0	61.5	63.7
Germany	61.8	74.8	81.8	84.0
Netherlands	–	45.0	68.0	72.0
New Zealand	52.0	56.0	59.0	–
Sweden	78.0	98.0	99.0	100.0
United Kingdom	–	–	–	83.0
United States	–	67.0	70.0	70.1

Source: OECD Environmental Data Compendium. 1985.

Table 51. **Water quality of Lake Biwa**

	Total phosphorous mg/litre			Total nitrogen mg/litre			
	1975	1980	1984	1970	1975	1980	1984
Biwa (North)	0.008	0.010	0.008	0.19	0.29	0.29	0.24
Biwa (South)	0.027	0.027	0.022	0.45	0.53	0.41	0.36

Source: OECD Environmental Data Compendium. 1983.

Mainly arising from motor vehicles, because of the high density, mixture with other uses and lightweight construction of traditional Japanese housing, noise is a major, mainly urban form of pollution. The number of motor vehicles in Japan has increased by over 40 times in the last 30 years to reach a total of 43 million in 1983. With the number of motor vehicles and their use both due to increase, a wide range of measures is needed in combination, including reducing noise emissions, tightening standards and their enforcement, supporting protective measures (such as noise barriers) and raising public understanding of the problems and ways to tackle them.

In particular urban planning and traffic management policies need to be integrated with environmental policies. Priority needs to be given to the improvement of areas fronting the main highway network, under the Improvement of Areas alongside Trunk Roads Act, 1980. By 1982 110 km of new road had benefitted in terms of reducing pollution and improved safety and appearance. 1 400 km of noise barriers and 4 000 km of tree planting had also been provided.

As for other forms of pollution, regular measurements of noise are taken at representative points throughout Japan. In 1982, of the 3843 measuring points at 585 (15 per cent) the appropriate environmental quality standards were met at all times, while at 103 (2.7 per cent) the standards were not reached at any of the four tested times. However, for 398 points where measurements were taken in 1979 and 1982, the level remained the same. The extent of the noise problem in Japan can be compared to other OECD countries for which figures are available (Table 52). A particular feature in Japan, dealt with an earlier chapter, is the high proportion of goods carried by road. In 1984 and 1985 exhaust and noise standards were tightened for large vehicles, motor cycles and diesel cars. These regulations will come into effect from 1986 and 1987. There is a priority programme of grants for the noise insulation of houses.

Table 52. **Population exposed to transport noise selected OECD countries, 1980**[1]

Percentage

Sound level[2]	⩾55	⩾60	⩾65	⩾70	⩾75
Japan[3]	80.0	58.0	31.0	10.0	1.0
Denmark	38.0	24.0	12.0	4.0	1.0
France	44.0	25.0	13.0	4.0	0.4
Germany	34.0	17.0	8.0	3.0	–
Netherlands	40.0	18.0	6.0	0.6	–
Sweden	38.0	24.0	11.0	4.0	1.0
United Kingdom	50.0	25.0	11.0	4.0	0.6
United States	37.0	18.0	7.0	2.0	0.4

1. See OECD Environmental Data Compendium, 1985, page 16 for detailed interpretation of this table.
2. Leq (dBA) outdoors.
3. OECD estimate.
Source: OECD Environmental Data Compendium 1985.

D. Policy Conclusions

Since the OECD Review of Environmental Policies in Japan was published in 1977, the nature of the urban, environmental challenges facing Japan has changed. Older, polluting heavy industries, which were the main concern of the report, have been replaced as the industrial structure of Japan has changed. New industrial sites tend to be located on inland, suburban sites served by road transport as opposed to coastal sites served by rail.

Parallel with these changes emphasis has shifted to pollution caused by day-to-day activities of the new urban population and the wastes – water and solid – produced. While the

"Absolute Liability" system, by which individual manufacturers are obliged to pay compensation for environmental damage, and the use of private sector funds to finance anti-pollution measures were applicable to industry, they are ineffective to deal with the current major challenge of domestic pollution. In the latter case, if the polluter pays principle is applied, it is individual households either directly through user charges or indirectly through taxation which will need to meet the costs. The major effort made to reduce industrial pollution shows that Japan has the means to achieve similar measures against new forms of pollution.

At the meeting of the OECD's Environment Committee at Ministerial level in June, 1985, the Japanese Minister of State for the Environment, in summarising the situation, said that "while the environmental condition in Japan has been, on the whole, showing some improvements, there are still some areas where improvements have been slow in coming, particularly in large metropolitan areas". The extension of environmental impact procedures would form an information base for identifying priorities for action.

Public opinion polls have indicated that there is concern over the standard of the environment. In a survey taken in 1982, almost one-third of the respondents indicated that priority needed to be given to environmental protection, as opposed to one-tenth who indicated economic growth as a priority. Two-fifths of the respondents considered that the two objectives could be pursued together. In terms of the major problems noise, followed by water pollution and air pollution, was ranked highest. These represent the priorities for action by the government, as also indicated by objective measures of noise levels and urban air and water quality.

Considerable action is being taken at the government level to make the public more aware of the importance of maintaining and improving environmental quality in towns. However, one particular area of concern is the present tendency to concentrate on renewal schemes of high rise flats. Although clearly there is a place for a proportion of high rise residential accommodation, alternative ways of both securing some open space and high density living need to be encouraged. This is particularly necessary in view of the importance of the right to sunshine in Japanese cultural values. Turning to the historic parts of Japanese cities, the urban conservation legislation that exists should be pursued more actively, together with the environmental enhancement of these areas.

NOTES AND REFERENCES

1. *Environmental Policies in Japan*, OECD, Paris, 1977.
2. The Environmental Protection Policy in Japan, K. Miyamoto in *Economic Growth and Resources: Problems related to Japan*, Ed. S. Tsuru, Macmillan Press, London, 1980.

Chapter 9

PERSPECTIVES ON URBAN POLICY

This final chapter assembles the policy conclusions from the previous chapters to present them as a unified set of perspectives on future urban policy in Japan.

Urban Japan

National urban policy aims to influence the location and quality of urban development and redevelopment. An urban perspective is particularly useful for integrating and targetting policies, particularly as cities are at the forefront of meeting the challenges and realising the opportunities arising from social and economic changes. This approach is recognised in Japan and the objectives of the City Planning Act, 1968 – to secure balanced development, the rational use of land, the promotion of public welfare and a healthy and cultured urban life – are a useful yardstick both to evaluate past performance and set priorities for future urban policies.

Japan is now a highly urbanised country and is destined to become more so, but this is not firmly established in the national consciousness. Because this high level of urbanisation has been achieved in a comparatively short period, it is not fully recognised in all spheres of government policy making. At the same time, two changes in the nature of the challenges facing urban policy makers are yet to be adequately recognised. First, a continuing need to cater for urban growth has to be balanced against the need for revitalisation in the urban areas so rapidly expanded in the past 40 years. Secondly, while the agricultural sector in Japan is still comparatively large, future urban development demands will come more from the natural increase of the existing urban population, linked to the process of urban deconcentration than from rural to urban migration, as in the past.

An additional contextual point of significance is the increasing difficulty and importance of making the right choice from amongst the urban policy options that are available. Most of urban Japan in the year 2000 is already built. At the same time, with falling rates both of national population growth and rural to urban migration, the development and redevelopment of one urban area will increasingly be at the expense of another. Although the overall shortage of good development land in Japan may prevent it occurring, the situation raises the risk of population and employment decline in those cities which are less well placed to compete.

Not only may increased inter-city competition lead to more central government involvement in urban policy, but the new link being made between urban development and stimulating domestic demand will make this involvement more likely. The Japanese government has now recognised the close link between domestic demand and the development and improvement of urban areas. To be effective, this will need to be reinforced by giving higher priority to urban policy and increasing the resources available to upgrade housing and the social capital in Japanese cities.

The Urban Policy Context

To be effective, urban policy needs to be integrated with a range of other policies. In the economic field a sustained rate of growth, combined with low inflation and low interest rates, provides a platform for increased expenditure on the implementation of urban policy. Public debt levels are comparatively high, but the high savings ratio and the prospect of continued economic growth suggest that more private investment will be available to support the expansion of domestic demand.

In particular, industrial policy needs to be closely allied to urban policy. Two important changes are taking place in the structure of Japanese industry. As in other comparable OECD countries the service sector is growing, but not at the expense of manufacturing which is maintaining its role. The primary sector is in decline but is still large and further contraction can be anticipated, particularly if agriculture becomes more efficient. The agricultural sector is itself one that has significant interactions with urban development. Both agricultural and urban policies have an interest in land resources, especially in and near the large metropolitan areas.

Another important trend, which is gaining momentum, will also affect future urban development. Policies towards the growth of leisure time, linked to the ageing of the population, will greatly influence the demands on certain types of urban facilities and services, particularly for recreation. These trends are likely to lead to more people spending more of their time in or near their homes. This will put a higher premium on the quality both of housing and of the neighbourhood environment. These concerns will need to be reflected in future urban policy priorities.

Urban policy making in Japan is becoming more complex. Increasing attention needs to be given to patterns of metropolitan migration, urban renovation and quality objectives, particularly in housing. These issues have been added to the more familiar list of concerns – national migration patterns, new urban development and quantitative aims, for example for infrastructure provision. A reassessment of policies often implies a review of policy institutions. In outline, what is required is one focus for urban policy formulation and implementation at national level and a new mechanism to ensure that urban policies and other related policies are evolved in harmony.

At the same time, to cope successfully with a more complex urban situation, more diversity of policy response will be required. This implies an active role for local government, with central government concentrating on achieving its own objectives and ensuring that local governments are provided with the necessary capability. The overall situation is one in which, rather than excessive central control, there is fragmentation of policy formulation and implementation. Also at the central level policy making co-ordination is not apparent.

For urban policies in Japan to improve their effectiveness in securing the objectives that have been set, a major initiative will need to be made to ensure that urban policy and other major policy areas are developed in unison. Utilising existing institutions, the National Land Agency is well placed to be developed into the forum for the co-ordination of urban policy with other central government policies. However, close links would be needed between the Agency and the Ministry of Construction with its responsibility for the initial formulation and eventual implementation of urban policy.

Balanced Development

In Japan the process of urban concentration at the national and metropolitan levels has been carried to a high degree when compared with other OECD countries. The first point is illustrated by the close proximity of the 3 major urban centres, the second by the high densities of Japanese cities. The two aspects of urban concentration have common roots in the rural to urban migration, reinforced by industrial growth policies, mainly in the 1950s and 1960s.

To achieve balanced development, broad policies on national development and land use planning are in place through successive updating of national plans and associated legislation. There is a consistent theme in these national policies in favour of the dispersal of industrial activity, based on the concept of growth poles coupled with restrictions on development in the major metropolitan areas. In practice economic and market forces, combined with the lack of strong instruments for implementation of national plans, have tended to intensify urban concentration in the metropolitan areas on the southern seaboard of central Honshu.

As a partial and more achievable alternative, some policy emphasis is now being given to dispersal within the metropolitan areas. The aim is to promote multi-centred cities with different functional characteristics, which might reduce some of the pressure on the older city centres. The success of this approach will depend on firm guidance and encouragement by national and local governments. In Tokyo, reducing the pressure for office development within the Yamanote line, by establishing sub-centres backed by incentives to develop there, is an urgent priority.

When the population figures are compared with the objectives of policy it can be seen that only now does a move towards a more balanced population structure seem to be emerging. In the period 1975-80 the population of all prefectures, except Tokyo with a 0.5 per cent decline, increased for the first time in the last 10 years. There are signs that industrial and urban policy are now working together to achieve balance, as opposed to earlier decades when despite the former policies concentration occurred.

The value of urban policies which pursue a consistent line in the long term has been shown. Industrial policy has changed to supporting growth sectors and "high tech" industries, which are seeking locations away from existing metropolitan areas. Existing deconcentration policies will need to be maintained accompanied by a switch of emphasis from the secondary to the tertiary sector. If this is not successful the probability is that the three metropolitan areas will become even more strongly differentiated from the rest of Japan. Already Tokyo has 27 per cent of all the tertiary employment in Japan.

The technopolises, building on a longstanding tradition of new towns, even if all fully implemented by 1990, would only cater for approximately 1%-2% of the Japanese population. However, signs exist that the central government may be willing to set an example by moving some of its functions from central Tokyo. Tsukuba new town shows what can be achieved in this respect. Other OECD countries have experience of policies offering financial incentives to companies which transfer offices from capital cities. These can particularly be successfully applied to non-headquarters type office functions.

The second major switch of emphasis, which again is already taking place but needs to be accelerated, is the restructuring of the metropolitan areas, now that growth will mainly come from within by natural increase. The accent, therefore, needs to be moved from national urban policies which were not successful in stopping unbalanced growth of Tokaido in the first place, to seeking balance within the Tokyo metropolitan area. Since 1975 Tokyo has strengthened its position in relation to Osaka and Nagoya and it is particularly in the national capital region that special measures need to be applied. A less centralised metropolitan structure, based on sub-centres either in or near Tokyo itself and the growth of medium-sized towns in the wider metropolitan area, will need to be supported by investment in the transportation infrastructure and social capital in the growing towns, to make them attractive alternatives to Tokyo.

Rational Use of Land

Japan is facing a period of urban deconcentration. To deal effectively with this process, involving both the construction of new development and the redevelopment of older areas, it needs to be handled in an orderly way. This can also help to ensure the efficient provision of urban infrastructure and to safeguard land resources, as well as to meet aspirations for an improved standard of urban living and environment. National public policy methods of seeking to secure the rational use of urban land can be divided into three categories, all of which are well represented in Japan. First, town planning legislation dealing with the development process, secondly, fiscal measures affecting the holding and sale of land and, thirdly, measures assisting the process of land assembly.

The Japanese Government has shown considerable ingenuity and persistence in pursuing the objective of the rational use of land. Radical departures from the current approach are not advocated, although changes to the agricultural support system and to the balance between rural and urban interests are needed, if the process of metropolitan development is to be handled effectively. With another 18 million urban residents to be housed by the year 2000 – almost two more cities the size of Tokyo – the urban policy challenges in Japan will not diminish. The main priority is to increase the supply of land in areas scheduled for development. As part of the 1985 economic measures to stimulate domestic demand, public sector sites suitable for development are to be released. The Government can continue to set an example in this respect.

To complement these measures, it is also important for policies to promote appropriate urban uses on vacant and agricultural land within Urbanisation Promotion Areas. In other areas urban containment policies are important for a number of reasons. They assist the efficient use of land and, by limiting random urban development, allow high quality agricultural land to be retained and good agricultural practices to be promoted. Urban policies and new measures such as Agricultural Promotion Areas have begun to assist urban containment. At the same time containment helps to prevent urban decline by limiting the choices for new development, ensuring that the regeneration of an existing urban area remains a competitive option.

However, within Urbanisation Control Areas there is a wide range of exemptions that are not controlled. The distinction between "promotion" and "control", even if it was more rigorously applied, is not sophisticated enough to achieve effective urban containment. A further refinement of the designations is needed to ensure that there are areas where there is an effective policy of no development. Institutional changes are less easy to evaluate. But it also seems that the procedures for land readjustment projects and for obtaining permission for development could be streamlined to increase land supply.

To achieve an improvement in the land supply situation, particularly underused land in the large metropolitan areas, action should be taken to identify such land and incentives introduced to bring it into effective urban use. To support these tax measures, central government should become more actively involved in securing and releasing land to the private sector and, more generally, monitoring the supply of land for urban development.

Changes of policy are also required to land and property taxation to support these urban planning measures. The tax on the holding of land that has been allocated for development needs to be progressively increased. This applies particularly in the three metropolitan areas. The increase in the rate of taxation on land holding needs to be complemented by the reduction of taxes which discourage the sale of land. These changes in taxation would initiate the land assembly process and make its subsequent progress easier.

A general property tax, reflecting the value of land, is a better way to secure the release of land and to stabilise land prices than a capital gains tax at the time the land is sold. However, owners might be encouraged to sell land in small parcels over a period of time to meet their tax obligations. Therefore, a minimum residential plot size needs to be introduced, which would also have the effect of improving housing standards, while not unduly influencing land prices and the amount of land required for urban development. A further change of approach is necessary to avoid the situation in which the smaller a development operation, the easier it is to avoid planning control. Also, charges need not rise proportionately with the complexity, duration and scale of the project as, for example, the proportion of land to be ceded free for public uses which currently increases with the area of site involved.

Housing and Urban Revitalisation

The Japanese government is pursuing a two-pronged approach in its drive for urban improvements. It is promoting decongestion by supporting the development of new towns at selected locations outside (but often closely associated with) existing metropolitan areas and by encouraging alternative sub-centres within the metropolitan areas. At the same time it is increasingly encouraging renewal of the older, overcrowded, inadequately serviced parts of the larger cities. There is a growing appreciation that current programmes, while certainly commendable and in many respects successful, are insufficient to match the speed of deterioration of the quality of life in the larger metropolitan areas. One response to this is an interest in securing an increased level of private investment in urban development and renewal programmes.

Redevelopment rather than restoration is the currently preferred option for improving older urban areas. A comprehensive project is easier to organise and can be implemented in one operation, once agreement and approval is secured. It usually allows too for a more orderly arrangement of streets and sites and for the provision of more open space, for recreational activity as well as disaster relief measures. Despite these advantages a greater emphasis on spontaneous renewal of existing properties on an individual basis could, if given more public sector support, usefully supplement and extend current redevelopment efforts. There is a very strong project approach to urban development in Japan. While the project response achieves speedy and highly visible results, a more exploratory examination of alternatives might suggest less costly and more satisfactory courses of action.

Land readjustment and other measures employed to implement urban redevelopment schemes have tended to produce a somewhat sterile and uninteresting townscape. "Grid-iron" street patterns and site division into rectangular building plots combined with a utilitarian building style may be the least-cost approach, but is generally devoid of variety. More recognition could be given to the animation and intricacy of the existing urban environment, where an inter-mixture of uses creates a vibrant atmosphere and a strong feeling of community inter-dependence. Redevelopment and renewal that combines some of the safety and efficiency of the new with the interest and variety of the old should be encouraged.

Production targets in recent housing programmes have not been achieved because demand did not reach the expected level and household formation rates were lower than predicted. To a very substantial degree housing demand in Japan relies on low-interest, long-term loans, which are not responsive to alterations in the overall economic situation. To fulfill policies which increase spending on housing to stimulate domestic demand, increasing diversity is needed in housing finance policies.

The goals set in the 1981-85 housing programme are aimed to ensure that, by 1986, no household would live in accommodation below the minimum housing standards. The overall economic development of Japan and the lack of policy priority and investment for housing have led to a slowdown in housing construction. In the light of the relatively low housing supply in Japan compared with other OECD countries, much higher priority needs to be devoted to housing if the Japanese housing supply is to be substantially improved. This is despite the fact that, measured by the relation between investment in housing to GDP, the performance of Japan compared with other OECD countries is favourable.

To maintain the demand for improved housing, the system of subsidies may need to be further reorientated to assist households during the initial years of house purchase. This would enable current private housing targets to be reached and for domestic demand to be boosted. The conditions of the most poorly housed sections of the population could be improved by putting more emphasis on the remodelling and repair of existing housing areas. The basis of housing policies should be further widened, to take into account urban environmental improvement and revitalisation considerations and to attract self-help resources. Also, the loss of population from inner urban areas of the larger cities would be reduced if more emphasis was given to improving older neighbourhoods.

In view of the importance of disaster reduction measures, a more sustained effort needs to be put into remodelling older areas and extending fire resistance treatment of existing buildings. Model schemes of low-rise high-density housing, as opposed to the recent stress on high rise schemes, should be encouraged to test their suitability in Japanese cities. These schemes should give more recognition to the qualities of variety and vitality found in the older areas of Japanese cities and more use should be made of traditional Japanese architectural styles and motifs.

Providing Urban Infrastructure

Public goods are part of the general welfare of a society and infrastructure and services for urban residents are an important part of social welfare. The stock of urban infrastructure in Japan is relatively small, both in comparison with the national standards that have been set and in international terms. Furthermore, the growth rate regarding investments in infrastructure is decreasing at the same time as the demand for infrastructure and services is increasing. There will be a continuing higher than average need for infrastructure investment in Japan, because of the requirements for disaster prevention and the low level of existing provision. In general, the larger cities and their hinterlands, which had to be rebuilt quickly 40 years ago and have since expanded considerably, have generally lower standards of infrastructure than elsewhere in Japan and will have the greatest future priorities.

Trends which are leading to further urbanisation in Japan, combined with increasing deconcentration in metropolitan areas, will continue to create demand for new urban infrastructure. A point not given as much attention as the question of quantity is the present and future need to maintain and improve the quality of the existing stock of infrastructure. When considerable resources must be used for the continuous expansion of infrastructure networks, there is a risk that the increasing needs for replacement, maintenance and improvement of the existing stock will be neglected. Examples from other OECD countries, where the quantity gaps are much smaller than in Japan, show that infrastructure maintenance and improvement present considerable challenges, especially if the general economic situation remains unchanged. With slower economic growth and restrictions on public capital investment, meeting maintenance and improvement needs becomes even more difficult.

In four specific sectors of infrastructure provision – urban road transport, sewerage and water supply, parks and open space, and disaster reduction – although progress has been made in the past two decades the rate has been extremely slow. The upgrading of standards of urban infrastructure, unless rates of spending increase sharply, will depend on a long-term sustained investment programme. In boosting domestic demand in Japan through the housing sector, this will itself create a demand for infrastructure which will also play a further part in boosting domestic demand.

As part of its economic policy, the government has established a tentative objective to lower the ratio of bond issues to expenditure and not to depend on deficit financing bonds after FY 1990. It is intended to keep public works bonds issues to the 1985/6 level of approximately Y 6 000 billion for the rest of the decade. However, if infrastructure investment is held steady in real terms, an increase in maintenance and replacement costs would limit new investment. A 3 per cent increase, which would have limited effect in the context of the comparatively small size of the public sector in Japan, would dramatically change the situation. This increase would need to come from the combined resources of central and local government, as well as the private sector.

Local government spending is more important in Japan than elsewhere in the OECD area, but local resources come in large measure from the national government. In a period of fiscal and financial restraint it is vital to target infrastructure spending to priority areas. One approach by the national government would be to reflect specific urban needs to a greater extent in allocating funds to local government. Secondly, more use could be made of the Fiscal Investment and Loan Programme to finance priority infrastructure spending. This would be in line with the Japanese Government's programme of stimulating domestic demand.

However, in view of the failure of past rates of infrastructure provision to keep up with short and long-term targets, more private resources will need to be devoted to investment in infrastructure. The means exists in Japan to bring this situation about without new legislation. In financing infrastructure and urban services there should be less emphasis on central government subventions, for both providers and users, and more emphasis on charges for use. Rises in land prices through infrastructure provision, particularly roads, should be recouped to pay for the facilities concerned. Also, more use should be made of procedures which secure infrastructure provision at no public cost, when it is provided by the developers of a project.

As the stock of existing urban infrastructure in Japan has rapidly increased in the last 40 years, more resources will need to be made available for modernisation and maintenance. Central government expenditure on urban development and allocations to local government and public agencies, should be more targetted on the basis of need, particularly to the three largest urban areas. To increase the general effectiveness of public investment, there should be better co-ordination of public expenditure on infrastructure provision and upgrading. In particular, the possibility of cross subsidies between new, profitable forms of infrastructure and other infrastructure, where direct charging is less easy, should be considered.

Urban Environment

Since the OECD Review of Environmental Policies in Japan was published in 1977, the nature of the urban, environmental challenges facing Japan has changed. Older, polluting heavy industries have been replaced as the industrial structure of Japan has changed. New industrial sites tend to be located on inland, suburban sites served by road transport, as opposed to coastal sites served by rail.

Parallel with these changes emphasis has shifted to pollution caused by day-to-day activities of the new urban population and the wastes – water and solid – produced. While the

"Absolute Liability" system, by which individual manufacturers are obliged to pay compensation for environmental damage, and the use of private sector funds to finance anti-pollution measures were applicable to industry, they are ineffective to deal with the current major challenge of domestic pollution. In the latter case, if the polluter pays principle is applied, it is individual households either directly through user charges or indirectly through taxation which will need to meet the costs. The major effort made to reduce industrial pollution shows that Japan has the means to achieve similar measures against new forms of pollution.

At the meeting of the OECD's Environment Committee at Ministerial level in June, 1985, the Japanese Minister of State for the Environment, in summarising the situation, said that "while the environmental condition in Japan has been, on the whole, showing some improvements, there are still some areas where improvements have been slow in coming, particularly in large metropolitan areas". The extension of environmental impact procedures would form an information base for identifying priorities for action.

Public opinion polls have indicated that there is concern over the standard of the environment. In a survey taken in 1982, almost one-third of the respondents indicated that priority needed to be given to environmental protection, as opposed to one-tenth who indicated economic growth as a priority. Two-fifths of the respondents considered that the two objectives could be pursued together. In terms of the major problems noise, followed by water pollution and air pollution, was ranked highest. These represent the priorities for action by the government, as also indicated by objective measures of urban air and water quality and noise levels.

Considerable action is being taken at the government level to make the public more aware of the importance of maintaining and improving environmental quality in towns. However, one particular area of concern is the present tendency to concentrate on renewal schemes of high rise flats. Although clearly there is a place for a proportion of high rise residential accommodation, alternative ways of both securing some open space and high density living need to be encouraged. This is particularly necessary in view of the importance of the right to sunshine in Japanese cultural values. Turning to the historic parts of Japanese cities, the urban conservation legislation that exists should be pursued more actively, together with the environmental enhancement of these areas.

OECD SALES AGENTS
DÉPOSITAIRES DES PUBLICATIONS DE L'OCDE

ARGENTINA - ARGENTINE
Carlos Hirsch S.R.L.,
Florida 165, 4° Piso,
(Galeria Guemes) 1333 Buenos Aires
Tel. 33.1787.2391 y 30.7122

AUSTRALIA-AUSTRALIE
D.A. Book (Aust.) Pty. Ltd.
11-13 Station Street (P.O. Box 163)
Mitcham, Vic. 3132   Tel. (03) 873 4411

AUSTRIA - AUTRICHE
OECD Publications and Information Centre,
4 Simrockstrasse,
5300 Bonn (Germany)   Tel. (0228) 21.60.45
Local Agent:
Gerold & Co., Graben 31, Wien 1 Tel. 52.22.35

BELGIUM - BELGIQUE
Jean de Lannoy, Service Publications OCDE,
avenue du Roi 202
B-1060 Bruxelles   Tel. 02/538.51.69

CANADA
Renouf Publishing Company Limited/
Éditions Renouf Limitée Head Office/
Siège social – Store/Magasin :
61, rue Sparks Street,
Ottawa, Ontario K1P 5A6
Tel. (613)238-8985. 1-800-267-4164
Store/Magasin : 211, rue Yonge Street,
Toronto, Ontario M5B 1M4.
Tel. (416)363-3171
Regional Sales Office/
Bureau des Ventes régional :
7575 Trans-Canada Hwy., Suite 305,
Saint-Laurent, Quebec H4T 1V6
Tel. (514)335-9274

DENMARK - DANEMARK
Munksgaard Export and Subscription Service
35, Nørre Søgade, DK-1370 København K
Tel. +45.1.12.85.70

FINLAND - FINLANDE
Akateeminen Kirjakauppa,
Keskuskatu 1, 00100 Helsinki 10   Tel. 0.12141

FRANCE
OCDE/OECD
Mail Orders/Commandes par correspondance :
2, rue André-Pascal,
75775 Paris Cedex 16
Tel. (1) 45.24.82.00
Bookshop/Librairie : 33, rue Octave-Feuillet
75016 Paris
Tel. (1) 45.24.81.67 or/ou (1) 45.24.81.81
Principal correspondant :
Librairie de l'Université,
12a, rue Nazareth,
13602 Aix-en-Provence   Tel. 42.26.18.08

GERMANY - ALLEMAGNE
OECD Publications and Information Centre,
4 Simrockstrasse,
5300 Bonn   Tel. (0228) 21.60.45

GREECE - GRÈCE
Librairie Kauffmann,
28, rue du Stade, 105 64 Athens Tel. 322.21.60

HONG KONG
Government Information Services,
Publications (Sales) Office,
Beaconsfield House, 4/F.,
Queen's Road Central

ICELAND - ISLANDE
Snæbjörn Jónsson & Co., h.f.,
Hafnarstræti 4 & 9,
P.O.B. 1131 – Reykjavik
Tel. 13133/14281/11936

INDIA - INDE
Oxford Book and Stationery Co.,
Scindia House, New Delhi 1   Tel. 45896
17 Park St., Calcutta 700016   Tel. 240832

INDONESIA - INDONESIE
Pdii-Lipi, P.O. Box 3065/JKT.Jakarta
Tel. 583467

ITALY - ITALIE
Libreria Commissionaria Sansoni,
Via Lamarmora 45, 50121 Firenze
Tel. 579751/584468
Via Bartolini 29, 20155 Milano   Tel. 365083
Sub-depositari :
Ugo Tassi, Via A. Farnese 28,
00192 Roma   Tel. 310590
Editrice e Libreria Herder,
Piazza Montecitorio 120, 00186 Roma
Tel. 6794628
Agenzia Libraria Pegaso,
Via de Romita 5, 70121 Bari
Tel. 540.105/540.195
Agenzia Libraria Pegaso, Via S.Anna dei
Lombardi 16, 80134 Napoli.   Tel. 314180
Libreria Hœpli,
Via Hœpli 5, 20121 Milano   Tel. 865446
Libreria Scientifica
Dott. Lucio de Biasio "Aeiou"
Via Meravigli 16, 20123 Milano   Tel. 807679
Libreria Zanichelli, Piazza Galvani 1/A,
40124 Bologna   Tel. 237389
Libreria Lattes,
Via Garibaldi 3, 10122 Torino   Tel. 519274
La diffusione delle edizioni OCSE è inoltre
assicurata dalle migliori librerie nelle città più
importanti.

JAPAN - JAPON
OECD Publications and Information Centre,
Landic Akasaka Bldg., 2-3-4 Akasaka,
Minato-ku, Tokyo 107   Tel. 586.2016

KOREA - CORÉE
Pan Korea Book Corporation
P.O.Box No. 101 Kwangwhamun, Seoul
Tel. 72.7369

LEBANON - LIBAN
Documenta Scientifica/Redico,
Edison Building, Bliss St.,
P.O.B. 5641, Beirut   Tel. 354429-344425

MALAYSIA - MALAISIE
University of Malaya Co-operative Bookshop
Ltd.,
P.O.Box 1127, Jalan Pantai Baru,
Kuala Lumpur   Tel. 577701/577072

NETHERLANDS - PAYS-BAS
Staatsuitgeverij
Chr. Plantijnstraat, 2 Postbus 20014
2500 EA S-Gravenhage   Tel. 070-789911
Voor bestellingen: Tel. 070-789880

NEW ZEALAND - NOUVELLE-ZÉLANDE
Government Printing Office Bookshops:
Auckland: Retail Bookshop, 25 Rutland Street,
Mail Orders, 85 Beach Road
Private Bag C.P.O.
Hamilton: Retail: Ward Street,
Mail Orders, P.O. Box 857
Wellington: Retail, Mulgrave Street, (Head
Office)
Cubacade World Trade Centre,
Mail Orders, Private Bag
Christchurch: Retail, 159 Hereford Street,
Mail Orders, Private Bag
Dunedin: Retail, Princes Street,
Mail Orders, P.O. Box 1104

NORWAY - NORVÈGE
Tanum-Karl Johan a.s
P.O. Box 1177 Sentrum, 0107 Oslo 1
Tel. (02) 801260

PAKISTAN
Mirza Book Agency
65 Shahrah Quaid-E-Azam, Lahore 3 Tel. 66839

PORTUGAL
Livraria Portugal,
Rua do Carmo 70-74, 1117 Lisboa Codex.
Tel. 360582/3

SINGAPORE - SINGAPOUR
Information Publications Pte Ltd
Pei-Fu Industrial Building,
24 New Industrial Road No. 02-06
Singapore 1953   Tel. 2831786, 2831798

SPAIN - ESPAGNE
Mundi-Prensa Libros, S.A.,
Castelló 37, Apartado 1223, Madrid-28001
Tel. 431.33.99
Libreria Bosch, Ronda Universidad 11,
Barcelona 7   Tel. 317.53.08/317.53.58

SWEDEN - SUÈDE
AB CE Fritzes Kungl. Hovbokhandel,
Box 16356, S 103 27 STH,
Regeringsgatan 12,
DS Stockholm   Tel. (08) 23.89.00
Subscription Agency/Abonnements:
Wennergren-Williams AB,
Box 30004, S104 25 Stockholm. Tel. 08/54.12.00

SWITZERLAND - SUISSE
OECD Publications and Information Centre,
4 Simrockstrasse,
5300 Bonn (Germany)   Tel. (0228) 21.60.45
Local Agent:
Librairie Payot,
6 rue Grenus, 1211 Genève 11
Tel. (022) 31.89.50

TAIWAN - FORMOSE
Good Faith Worldwide Int'l Co., Ltd.
9th floor, No. 118, Sec.2
Chung Hsiao E. Road
Taipei   Tel. 391.7396/391.7397

THAILAND - THAILANDE
Suksit Siam Co., Ltd.,
1715 Rama IV Rd.,
Samyam Bangkok 5   Tel. 2511630

TURKEY - TURQUIE
Kültur Yayinlari Is-Türk Ltd. Sti.
Atatürk Bulvari No: 191/Kat. 21
Kavaklidere/Ankara   Tel. 25.07.60
Dolmabahce Cad. No: 29
Besiktas/Istanbul   Tel. 160.71.88

UNITED KINGDOM - ROYAUME UNI
H.M. Stationery Office,
Postal orders only:
P.O.B. 276, London SW8 5DT
Telephone orders: (01) 622.3316, or
Personal callers:
49 High Holborn, London WC1V 6HB
Branches at: Belfast, Birmingham,
Bristol, Edinburgh, Manchester

UNITED STATES - ÉTATS-UNIS
OECD Publications and Information Centre,
Suite 1207, 1750 Pennsylvania Ave., N.W.,
Washington, D.C. 20006 - 4582
Tel. (202) 724.1857

VENEZUELA
Libreria del Este,
Avda F. Miranda 52, Aptdo. 60337,
Edificio Galipan, Caracas 106
Tel. 32.23.01/33.26.04/31.58.38

YUGOSLAVIA - YOUGOSLAVIE
Jugoslovenska Knjiga, Knez Mihajlova 2,
P.O.B. 36, Beograd   Tel. 621.992

Orders and inquiries from countries where Sales
Agents have not yet been appointed should be sent
to:
OECD, Publications Service, Sales and
Distribution Division, 2, rue André-Pascal, 75775
PARIS CEDEX 16.

Les commandes provenant de pays où l'OCDE n'a
pas encore désigné de dépositaire peuvent être
adressées à :
OCDE, Service des Publications. Division des
Ventes et Distribution. 2. rue André-Pascal. 75775
PARIS CEDEX 16.

70062-09-1986

OECD PUBLICATIONS, 2, rue André-Pascal, 75775 PARIS CEDEX 16 - No. 43751 1986
PRINTED IN FRANCE
(97 86 05 1) ISBN 92-64-12886-7